Bible Numbers & Symbols

WARREN HENDERSON

All Scripture quotations are from the New King James Version of the Bible, unless otherwise noted. Copyright © 1982 by Thomas Nelson, Inc. Nashville, TN

Bible Numbers and Symbols

By Warren Henderson
Copyright © 2022

Cover Design: Ben Bredeweg
Editing/Proofreading: Dan Macy and David Lindstrom

Published by Warren A. Henderson
1025 Iron Cap Drive
Stevensville, MT 59870

Perfect Bound ISBN: 978-1-939770-70-7
eBook ISBN: 978-1-939770-71-4

ORDERING INFORMATION:
Copies of *Bible Numbers and Symbols* are available through various online retailers worldwide. Our website address is: warrenahendersonpublishing.com

Table of Contents

PREFACE — 1

THE BENEFIT OF UNIFORMITY — 3

    The Reason for Metaphor — 4
    The Principle of First-mention — 5
    Proper Numerical Hermeneutics — 6
    Numerals in the Bible — 9
    Biblical Arithmetic — 10
    The Significance of Uniformity — 12

BIBLICAL NUMBERS — 13

    One – Unity, Independence, and Supremacy — 13
    Two – Difference, Union, and Testimony — 14
    Three – Completeness, Perfection, and Resurrection — 15
    Four – Earthly Order — 17
    Five – Divine Grace and Goodness — 19
    Six – Man's Weakness and Sin, Satan's Evil — 21
    Seven – Spiritual Perfection and Completeness — 22
    Eight – New Beginnings — 24
    Nine – Finality and Spiritual Fruitfulness — 25
    Ten – Divine Order and Responsibility — 27
    Eleven – Judgment and Disorder — 28
    Twelve – Governmental Perfection — 30
    Thirteen – Rebellion and Depravity — 31
    Fourteen – Deliverance and Salvation — 32
    Fifteen – Rest — 34
    Sixteen – Love — 35
    Seventeen – Victory — 37
    Eighteen – Bondage — 40
    Nineteen – Faith — 42
    Twenty – Redemption — 43
    Twenty-one – Wickedness and Sinfulness — 45
    Twenty-two – Light — 47
    Twenty-three – Death — 49

Twenty-four – The Priesthood	51
Twenty-five – Forgiveness of Sins	52
Twenty-six – Gospel Testimony	53
Twenty-seven – Gospel Preaching	54
Twenty-eight – Eternal Life	55
Twenty-nine – Departure	56
Thirty – Dedication and the Offering of Christ's Blood	57
Thirty-one – Offspring	59
Thirty-two – A Vow, Promise, or Covenant	60
Thirty-three – Returning or the Hope of Resurrection	61
Thirty-four – Consecration or Naming a Son	62
Thirty-five – Hope	63
Thirty-six – An Enemy or Adversary	64
Thirty-seven – God's Word	65
Thirty-eight – Bondage	67
Thirty-nine – Sorrow and Suffering	68
Forty – Probation and Testing	69

OTHER UNIQUE NUMBERS — 71

Seventy – The Jewish Nation of Israel	71
One Hundred Twenty-Seven – Israel's Rejection of Christ and Resulting Blindness	72
One Hundred Fifty-Three – Abundant Blessing	75
Two Hundred Seventy-Six – Sovereign Control	76
Six Hundred Sixty-Six – The Number of the Antichrist	77

BIBLICAL METAPHOR — 79

Heavenly Creatures	79
Earthly Creatures in Sacrifice	81
Other Earthly Creatures	84
Metals and Materials	87
Colors	90
Miscellaneous	92

A TRIUNE GOD IN METAPHOR — 105

ENDNOTES — 109

Other Books by the Author

A Heart for God – A Devotional Study of 1 and 2 Samuel

Afterlife – What Will It Be Like?

Answer the Call – Finding Life's Purpose

Be Holy and Come Near– A Devotional Study of Leviticus

Behold the Saviour

Be Angry and Sin Not

Conquest and the Life of Rest – A Devotional Study of Joshua

Door of Hope – A Devotional Study of the Minor Prophets

Exploring the Pauline Epistles

Forsaken, Forgotten, and Forgiven – A Devotional Study of Jeremiah

Glories Seen & Unseen

Hallowed Be Thy Name – Revering Christ in a Casual World

Hiding God – The Ambition of World Religion

In Search of God – A Quest for Truth

Infidelity and Loyalty – A Devotional Study of Ezekiel and Daniel

Israel's Kings – A Devotional Study of Kings and Chronicles

Knowing the All-Knowing

Managing Anger God's Way

May We See Christ? – A New Testament Journey

May We See Christ? – An Old Testament Journey

May We Serve Christ? – A New Testament Journey
May We Serve Christ? – An Old Testament Journey
Mind Frames – Where Life's Battle Is Won or Lost
Out of Egypt – A Devotional Study of Exodus
Overcoming Your Bully
Passing the Torch – Mentoring the Next Generation for Christ
Relativity and Redemption – A Devotional Study of Judges and Ruth
Revive Us Again – A Devotional Study of Ezra, Nehemiah, and Esther
Seeds of Destiny – A Devotional Study of Genesis
Sorrow and Comfort – A Devotional Study of Isaiah
The Beginning of Wisdom – A Devotional Study of Job, Psalms, Proverbs, Ecclesiastes, and Song of Solomon
The Bible: Myth or Divine Truth?
The Evil Nexus – Are You Aiding the Enemy?
The Fruitful Bough – Affirming Biblical Manhood
The Fruitful Vine – Celebrating Biblical Womanhood
The Hope of Glory – A Preview of Things to Come
The Olive Plants – Raising Spiritual Children
Your Home the Birthing Place of Heaven

Henderson Publishing YouTube Channel

Preface

All that we observe in the celestial heavens above or in our terrestrial home below is governed by mathematical order. Orbits, rotations, dimensions, densities, chemical processes, energy conversions, spectra of wave energies and particle emissions, and the continuance of life over the eons of time all declare an arithmetical intellect. Moreover, this genius Mastermind knows and controls all things.

Our Designer also understands our natural limitations to comprehend spiritual matters. While He does use a variety of means to call our attention to Himself, such as our human conscience and the testimony of His creation, He has more specifically written down what He wants us to understand. In doing so, God has employed a variety of literary forms to reveal Himself and His Christ-centered plan of redemption to us. These include word pictures, prophecies, shadows, types, allegories, symbols, numerical ideas, and, obviously, plain language. The One who maintains the universe in perfect order likewise expresses such order in what He says. David declares, God's *way* is perfect (Ps. 18:30), and so is His *Word* (Ps. 19:7). All that God expresses in word is a reflection of His holy character, His perfect order, and His sovereign control.

The Bible is God's preserved communication to humanity. Paul tells us that Scripture is literally God-breathed (2 Tim. 3:16-17). Peter says that, *"holy men of God spoke as they were moved by the Holy Spirit"* (2 Pet. 1:20-21). This means that all Scripture, in all of its various literary forms, is divine in origin and profitable for us to heed. God's truth is contained in the whole of Scripture, which means that in order to understand what God is saying to us, we must use Scripture to interpret Scripture. Only when we have an interpretation of a passage that agrees with all of Scripture have we discerned what God means (i.e., the truth).

It is necessary for human language to incorporate numerical expression to convey ideas. God uses numbers in Scripture for the same reason. Obviously, the primary use of biblical numbers is to convey a literal meaning of quantity. Seldom does the Bible state that a number is to be interpreted in a figurative sense, instead of a mathematical expression. The number associated with the mark of the beast, *666*, would be an example of such a rare instance, as *six* refers to *the number of man* (Rev. 13:18). The number 666 represents something that is complete, but that did not originate with God. It is man under the apex of satanic control; Paul refers to this as the "mystery of lawlessness."

If the primary meaning of biblical numbers is quantity, then we need to be careful in applying a figurative sense, lest we negate their intended idea. With that said, a symbolic concept may coexist with a literal numerical meaning, but in a less prominent way. A figurative meaning may be inferred from the biblical text, if frequent and consistent associations between that specific number and an idea are observed.

This method of inference is used to derive biblical typology in some instances. An Old Testament *type* of Christ is generally verified by New Testament Scripture (e.g., John 3:14-15), but this is not always the case. For instance, the New Testament does not specifically validate Joseph as a type of Christ, but the dozens of similarities between Joseph's circumstances and those relating to Christ confirm that Joseph is a genuine prophetic foreshadow of Christ (as Stephen assumes in Acts 7).

Similarly, if a specific number is repeatedly tied to a consistent idea in Scripture, we may safely conclude that God is conveying additional information to us to further emphasize something in the narrative or to highlight some aspect of His purposes. This less-apparent revelation in numbers, however, will not introduce anything new or contrary to what the plain language of Scripture affirms. With this premise stated, numbers *one* through *fourteen, twenty, twenty-four, thirty, forty*, and *seventy* do have enough observable frequency and consistent usage to determine their metaphorical meanings with high confidence.

The figurative meanings of other numbers less than forty in Scripture are more challenging to discern, and in a handful of cases, the evidence is admittedly inconclusive. Accordingly, a rigid assessment should be avoided. Caution is warranted in evaluating these cases, as we do not want to be guilty of affixing an idea to a number apart from God's design. A likely meaning for these numbers will be suggested as based on the available evidence and the use of *Bible Mathematics*. *Bible Mathematics* infers that the meanings of these less-frequent larger numbers can be grasped by the combined meanings of the smaller, understood numbers.

The whole of Scripture forms the basis of understanding the literal and figurative meanings contained in any particular passage. It is God's consistent use of numbers and symbols throughout Scripture that permits us to discover the various layers of truth revealed in Scripture; these He desires us to know and to appreciate.

The Benefit of Uniformity

There are several unique facets which testify of Scripture's supernatural origin. The Bible's prolific prophetic content, textual authenticity, scientific conformity, and textual uniformity are examples, to name a few. The Bible was written over a 1,600-year period by some forty different writers who were from various social backgrounds and geographical locations, yet uniform content is displayed throughout. Often the Old Testament prophets did not fully understand the meaning of the very words they uttered on God's behalf (1 Pet. 1:10-12). This fact puts the Bible in stark contrast with the "holy books" of world religions, which are often composed by one individual – a religious founder.

How was such marvelous uniformity maintained in one collection of so many different writings, by so many different writers, and over so many centuries? The only answer to this question is that one entity controlled the entire expression of thought. God controlled the speech and pens of the prophets and the apostles (2 Tim. 3:16). Scripture, then, is a direct expression of both His truth and His love to mankind. The Bible reveals God's supreme gift of love – His own Son to the world (John 3:16). Thus, the uniform focus of the Bible centers in the progressive revealing of God's purposes that culminate in the incarnation, life, death, and resurrection of Christ.

Bible uniformity permits us to examine the whole of Scripture to discover the consistent metaphoric meanings that God assigns to numbers, colors, creatures, objects, etc. Obviously, most of Scripture has a literal meaning, but especially in prophetic or typological portions of the Bible there is more information being revealed to us than the plain grammatical sense.

For example, the Holy Spirit's usage of *types* in the Old Testament is extensive. By the word *type*, we simply mean a picture, figure, or pattern that reflects something or someone in reality (which is the antitype). The word "type" comes from the Greek word *tupos*, meaning, "print." It is used to speak of the nail "print" in the Lord's hand (John 20:25) and of the tabernacle furniture which was to be fashioned according to the "pattern" given Moses in the mount (Heb. 8:5). There are literally hundreds of types of Christ contained within the Old

Testament. These are identified and illuminated by New Testament truth for our benefit.

The Reason for Metaphor

A metaphor is a word or phrase used in place of another to suggest an analogy or likeness between them. For example, the Lord Jesus said, *"I am the living bread which came down from heaven. If anyone eats of this bread, he will live forever; and the bread that I shall give is My flesh, which I shall give for the life of the world"* (John 6:51). The Lord had already explained to His audience the meaning of the metaphor, that is, how to eat the life-giving bread that He was offering them: *"I am the bread of life. He who comes to Me shall never hunger, and he who believes in Me shall never thirst. But I said to you that you have seen Me and yet do not believe"* (John 6:35). In the same way that one chooses to eat bread to live, each person must believe on Christ to receive the eternal life that He offers.

The Old Testament especially is full of metaphoric and typological expressions. Why did the Spirit of God inspire the pens of the writers to include so much figurative language within the historical narratives, the poetic expressions, and the prophetic declarations of the Old Testament? Undoubtedly, God has chosen to craft Scripture in such a way, as to uphold the main theme of the Bible from cover to cover. John 3:16 concisely expresses the central idea of Scripture: *"For God so loved the world that He gave His only begotten Son, that whoever believes in Him should not perish but have everlasting life."* Jesus Christ is the main theme of the Bible: *"For the testimony of Jesus is the spirit of prophecy"* (Rev. 19:10). *"For all the promises of God in Him [Christ] are Yes, and in Him Amen"* (2 Cor. 1:20).

Yet, it was necessary to keep the plan of salvation in Christ a mystery until after His death and resurrection, otherwise those opposing God would not have crucified Him, that is, if God's plan for showing mercy to humanity had been known (1 Cor. 2:7-8). This is why the messianic prophecies concerning Christ are generally scattered, seemingly sporadically, throughout the Old Testament. The truth was declared, yet in such a way that full understanding of the events and benefits of Calvary would not be understood from just one text. This is why much of the Old Testament pictures of Christ are concealed in abstract symbols, reclusive personal portraits, and mysterious names. Though these Old Testament gems were once concealed from human comprehension, they accentuate Christ when illuminated by the light of New Testament revelation.

As one investigates the Old Testament with the light of the New Testament, these abundant pictures and types of Christ are understood. Volumes of books have been written on these striking preludes of realities to come. It is no exaggeration to state that hundreds of pictures and shadows of Christ are contained in the Old Testament.

The uniform and repetitive use of colors, metals, materials, objects, creatures, people, and numbers throughout the Bible demonstrates that all Scripture came from one Mind – God, Himself. Through the observed consistency of symbolic meanings in Scripture and the revelation of the New Testament, we are able to understand Old Testament types and metaphor with a high degree of accuracy.

The Principle of First Mention

This hermeneutical principle implies that the first mention of a particular key word in the Bible establishes that word's general application throughout Scripture. Here are a few examples of this principle at work in Scripture.

We find the key words of "seven" and "sanctified" initially occurring in Genesis 2:1-3. The number *seven* is here introduced as God's number and hence becomes a fundamental building block throughout Scripture of things that pertain to Him. God speaks of completeness or perfection through the number seven. The word "sanctified" means "set apart" or "holy." The week of creation ended with a day of rest for the Lord. This was not a divine response to weariness, but to satisfaction (Isa. 40:28). Although God did not command mankind to keep the Sabbath at this time, He taught, through example, the principle of resting one day in seven. Later, He would command that the seventh day be "set apart" by the children of Israel (Ex. 20:8-11, 23:10-12, 31:13-17) although they would miserably fail to do so.

Another good example of the principle of first mention is found in Genesis 15. God performed no signs and wonders in this chapter, but simply reaffirms His promise to Abram of a natural son through his wife Sarai. That was good enough for Abram – he simply trusted God and believed. God responded by accrediting a standing of righteousness to Abram's account. This accrediting, or accounting, of divine righteousness to a sinner exercising faith is seen throughout the Bible and is thoroughly explained by the Apostle Paul in Romans 4 and 5. Obviously, God wanted no confusion on this matter, for the words "believe," "counted," and "righteousness" all occur for the first time in the Bible in one verse, and in one Divine declaration: *"And he believed in the LORD, and He accounted it to him for righteousness"* (Gen. 15:6), just after the first reference to "the word of the Lord" in the Bible (Gen. 15:1). Faith is the ability of the soul to reach beyond what can be verified by the human senses and trust what he cannot confirm by his own understanding. One must have this kind of faith to be justified in Christ and to please God, *"for without faith it is impossible to please Him"* (Heb. 11:6).

A third example of the principle of first mention is observed in Genesis 22. The English words "love," "worship," and "lamb" first occur in Genesis 22. Twice previously, the Hebrew word *shachah* was translated "bowed," but this is the first time it is associated with "worship" through sacrifice in Scripture. The initial meanings of love, worship, and selfless sacrifice are there defined and then developed throughout the remainder of the Bible. The whole of Scripture teaches us that there can be no true worship without love and there can be no true love without God's Lamb – the Lord Jesus Christ.

Proper Numerical Hermeneutics

It must be emphasized that we must interpret God's Word literally, unless there is a good reason not to. In some instances, the passage informs us that the text has a figurative sense, but the numbers within the narrative should be taken literally. For example, Pharaoh's two dreams, which Joseph interpreted, were a figurative representation of future events (Gen. 41:14-32). However, the seven fat cows and seven gaunt cows within Pharaoh's dream represented two different and literal seven-year periods in the future. The following principles are offered to assess whether or not a passage should be considered in the figurative sense.

a. Use the figurative sense if a literal meaning is impossible or absurd. For example, it would be absurd to think that the head of the Lord Jesus literally has seven eyes and seven horns; rather, these facets represent His attributes of omniscience and omnipotence (Rev. 5:6).

b. Use the figurative sense if the expression is an obvious figure of speech or idiom. For example, the term "one day and one night" was a Jewish idiom indicating a day, even when only a part of a day was indicated (e.g., Gen. 42:74; 1 Sam. 30:12). Hence, the term "three days and nights" and "three days" were common expressions the Jews used interchangeably (e.g., Matt. 16:21; Mark 8:31). The phrase "three days and nights" should not be taken literally, but rather figurative of any portion of three days.

c. Use the figurative sense when figures of speech only make sense when read figuratively. John describes the immense throng of redeemed saints and angelic beings gathered around God's throne to praise the Lamb: *"the number of them was ten thousand times ten thousand, and thousands of thousands"* (Rev. 5:11). The largest number in the Greek language was a myriad, so John imposes a figurative expression to indicate that those gathered around God's throne were innumerable – an indefinite number. John was not expecting us to perform a mathematical analysis of his statement to calculate the actual number of worshipers.

d. Use the figurative sense when the number is being used as a hyperbolic expression. A hyperbole is a figure of speech that exaggerates the thought for emphasis and effect. In the parable of *The Unforgiving Servant* (Matt. 18:23-35), a servant was forgiven an enormous debt of 10,000 talents (worth several billion dollars in today's market) because he pled for mercy before the king. Afterwards, however, this same servant did not show compassion to a fellow servant who owed him one hundred denarii (less than $100). Literally speaking, there is no way that a servant could compile a debt of 10,000 talents; the total tax levied on Palestine by the Romans during the time of Christ was 800 talents per year. The number of 10,000 is purposely exaggerated to better illustrate the infinite compassion of God towards those who genuinely seek Him for mercy.

e. Use the figurative sense if the number is clearly being used as a metaphor. Metaphor uses words and numbers in place of something else to suggest an analogy or likeness between them. The night before His crucifixion, the Lord Jesus asked His Father to grant oneness to all those who would later trust Him for salvation: *"that they may be one just as We are one: I in them, and You in Me; that they may be made perfect in one"* (John 17:22-23). Clearly the Lord is using the number *one* to express the idea of perfect union and unity (i.e., divine oneness).

f. Use the figurative sense if a literal interpretation goes contrary to the context of the passage. For example, the Lord was not telling Peter to extend forgiveness to another up to and including 490 instances (Matt. 18:22). Rather, by employing the multiplication of the numbers *seven* and *seventy*, the Lord was telling Peter that he should be completely characterized by a forgiving (a releasing) spirit.

g. Use the figurative sense if the literal interpretation would contradict sound doctrine. In Proverbs 6:16-19, Solomon reminds his son of seven things that God hates: a proud look, a lying tongue, murder, devising wicked schemes, a swift inclination to do mischief, a false witness, and those who sow discord among God's people. This does not mean that God only hates these particular sins; God loathes all behavior and thinking that opposes His holy character. These abominations include one sin of attitude, one of thought, two of speech, two of action, and one of influence, showing that the full product of the first six sins results in the latter offense of discord and division. The sentence construction connects the number *seven* (to symbolize completeness) with needless division and discord among God's people to indicate that this is something that God really hates!

Lastly, we should remember that the order of books within the Old Testament and New Testament Canons was humanly arranged. Likewise, the individual book divisions into chapters and verses occurred centuries after the direct revelation from God was received. Although the canonical arrangement of biblical books and the chapter/verse divisions of these books are beneficial, these were not divinely inspired. Therefore, there should be no reliance on humanly devised order or division of Scripture to determine a figurative meaning of numbers in Scripture.

Numerals in the Bible

Many Christians do not realize that the numerals that represent numbers in Scripture today were not incorporated into our Bibles until centuries after the books of the Bible were canonized. In the original autographs, biblical numbers were spelled out with letters symbolically representing various numbers. In ancient times this representation of number by letters was called a *gematria*. Every letter in both the Hebrew and Greek alphabets has a numerical meaning. This permitted the expression of numbers by using letters and combinations of letters which, in total, created the subject value. Dr. Ed F. Vallowe provides this overview of the Hebrew and Greek systems for expressing quantities[1]:

THE HEBREW ALPHABET

consists of 22 (2 x 11) letters, so the 5 finals were added to make up three series of 9, or 27 in all, but are not used in Gematria.

Aleph א = 1	Yod י = 10	Koph ק = 100
Beth ב = 2	Kaph כ = 20	Resh ר = 200
Gimel ג = 3	Lamed ל = 30	Shin ש = 300
Daleth ד = 4	Mem מ = 40	Tau ת = 400
He ה = 5	Nun נ = 50	Kaph ך = 500
Vau ו = 6	Samech ס = 60	Mem ם = 600
Zayin ז = 7	Ayin ע = 70	Nun ן = 700
Cheth ח = 8	Pe פ = 80	Pe ף = 800
Teth ט = 9	Tsaddi צ = 90	Tsaddi ץ = 900

(Finals.)

THE GREEK ALPHABET

The Greek letters were 24, and the required number, 27, was made up by using the final "s" or ς (called Stigma) for 6, and adding two arbitrary symbols called Koppa, for 90, and Sampsi, for 900.

Alpha α = 1	Iota ι = 10	Rho ρ = 100
Beta β = 2	Kappa κ = 20	Sigma σ = 200
Gamma γ = 3	Lambda λ = 30	Tau τ = 300
Delta δ = 4	Mu μ = 40	Upsilon υ = 400
Epsilon ε = 5	Nu ν = 50	Phi φ = 500
Stigma ςº = 6	Xi ξ = 60	Chi χ = 600
Zeta ζ = 7	Omicron ο = 70	Psi ψ = 700
Eta η = 8	Pi π = 80	Omega ω = 800
Theta θ = 9	*Koppa* ϙ = 90	*Sampsi* ϡ = 900

Egypt, Greece, and Rome used the decimal system for numbers (i.e., numbers were expressed in base ten). The Hebrews did not use a decimal system, which makes determining a number or its mathematical expression of quantity more cumbersome. A *numeral* is a symbol used to represent a specific number of something. If someone wins a 10K footrace, we understand that the distance ran was 10,000 meters; "K" is a symbol representing 1,000. The symbol "M" represents 1,000 in the Roman numbering system.

The gematric expressions in Scripture (i.e., a series of letters representing numbers), in some cases, were quite long and contributed to some copying errors through the centuries. For example, about one-sixth of the numbers in 1 and 2 Kings, when compared to parallel accounts in 1 and 2 Chronicles, do not agree. Most of these errors are obvious and certainly do not undermine the meaning of the text. For example, it would be logical to conclude that only seventy men from the small village of Beth Shemesh died for the offense of peering into the Ark of the Covenant, in lieu of 50,070 (1 Sam. 6:19). The Bible has been scientifically proven to be 99.5 percent authentic to the original autographs which were inspired by God.[2] The truth of God's Word is in the whole and Scripture tests itself for accuracy.

Biblical Arithmetic

The number *one* is not a prime number, because it does not have only two positive factors; yet, it is a prime number scriptural speaking. The numbers *two* and *three* are prime numbers in both the mathematical and the scriptural sense. The numbers *one*, *two* and *three* are therefore distinct from those numerals which follow them and, in fact, become the building blocks for larger numbers. The numbers *five* and *seven* are also prime numbers in mathematics, but this is not true scripturally speaking.

For example, the number *four* is equally dividable by the number *two*, but Scripture normally creates the number *four* by adding *three* and *one* together. The number *five* is usually achieved by adding *one* and *four* together and the number *seven* is achieved by adding *three* and *four* together. All this to say that there is a stark difference between the numbers one, two, and three and those numbers which follow. The latter often have a manufactured and composite meaning as derived by the combinations of the lesser numbers used to derive them.

The Benefit of Uniformity

Consider the four Gospel accounts in the New Testament. By devising a *three and one* Gospel format, God has upheld the symbolic scriptural meanings of the number *one* and *three* to represent His Son to the world. Number *one* represents divine unity and speaks of the Creator, while the number *three* signifies divine fullness and perfection. God used two numbers pertaining to Himself to manifest the divine glory of His Son in the Gospels. Hence, we have the three synoptic Gospel accounts (Matthew, Mark, and Luke) and John, which is unique from the other records.

The number *five* may be achieved by adding *two* and *three* together or by adding *one* and *four* together, which is more common, scripturally speaking. For example, the Lord did use the number *two*, symbolizing division, and the number *three*, representing completeness, to foretell of the comprehensive and decisive outcome that trusting in Him would have among friends and family (Luke 12:52). However, the figurative meaning of *five* is more commonly obtained by combining the numbers *one* and *four* together. *One* speaks of our all-sufficient God, while *four* declares His creative work as pertaining to man (i.e., earthly order). Through the all-sufficient redemptive work of God, He is able to offer *grace* to man, though mankind corrupted His creative work by sin in Eden. In the five books of the Law, God reveals man's failure in Genesis and His remedy, substitutional death of a perfect sacrifice for the guilty, in the next four books (Exodus-Deuteronomy).

Concerning the number *seven*, God normally uses the number *three*, symbolizing divine perfection with the number *four* to speak of earthly order. *Seven* parables revealing the mysteries of *the Kingdom of Heaven* are found in Matthew 13. The first *four* parables were spoken to a crowd composed of both believers and non-believers. In each of these first *four* parables, an enemy is present to oppose God's efforts of expanding His kingdom on Earth. However, the last *three* parables were told privately to the Lord's disciples and no enemy is presented in the narrative of these stories. In these last *three* parables, the Lord reveals how God is able to save Israel, the Church, and Gentiles during the Tribulation Period despite Satan's previous efforts to thwart the work of God. The numbers *three* and *four* are used to signify that God's work of redemption on the Earth will be complete and perfect.

It is through God's unusual division of numbers that He employs significance to a number. He combines the meanings of lesser numbers to create the importance of a large number. The difference between the first *three* numbers and those that follow is the significance between what is scripturally primitive and what obtains a manufactured meaning.

The Significance of Uniformity

Uniformity is a necessary part of any discipline of science. One must expect that doing exactly the same experiment twice will give the same results or the order of things cannot be understood. Science assumes that there is a general uniformity in nature. The same understanding is true concerning the study of the Bible's numbers and metaphors. Because God consistently applies the same figurative idea to objects, creatures, and numbers throughout Scripture, we can derive His intended meaning of these. This can be the only basis for obtaining an accurate meaning of numbers in the Bible. F. W. Grant states:

> The God of nature uses things according to their nature. He does not use water to regenerate a soul. He does not change bread into something that to look and touch and taste remains the same, but is not. And so the spiritual meaning of the numerals also has its roots in nature. This rule observed helps greatly to restrain the mere lawlessness of the imagination, of which we do well to be afraid. We can hardly go astray when all meanings of the number *one* must come under its cardinal form as *unity*, or under its ordinal, as *primacy*.[3]

It is usually people who know little about the Bible who identify supposed contradictions in the Bible. Either these individuals lack an understanding of a passage's correct context or they are not applying proper hermeneutics to interpret its true meaning. Besides the divine message contained in the normal narrative, God often uses numbers, symbols, metals, colors, names, etc. to convey complementary ideas. These more abstract forms of revelation do not substitute for or supplement the clear teaching of Scripture, but rather reiterate the obvious message of Scripture through metaphor.

The consistent use of symbols, numbers, analogies, names, first-mention occurrences, fulfilled prophetic types and shadows, plus the plain and consistent teachings of the Bible prove it to be the orchestrated genius of one Mind – the Bible is God's oracle of truth to humanity!

Biblical Numbers

In Scripture, most numbers have a literal meaning (e.g., Christ arose from the grave on the *third* day), but some numbers serve a figurative purpose. We understand that the Lamb (Jesus Christ) with *seven* horns in Revelation 5:6 symbolically represents the Son of God's omnipotence, because in Scripture *seven* is the number of *perfection*, and a *horn* represents *power*.

Sometimes both a figurative and a literal meaning may be intended, especially when the obvious literal sense is within a personal narrative and the figurative sense conveys a future meaning verified elsewhere in Scripture. For example, the seven-year famine in Joseph's day was both an actual devastating famine that affected the whole land and also a forewarning of a yet future seven-year Tribulation Period that will devastate the entire planet (Dan. 9:27). So, without undermining the plain meaning of the text, God applies, generally speaking, a consistent metaphoric meaning for numbers in Scripture. In this chapter, we will investigate numbers *one* through *forty*. In the next chapter, several numbers over *forty* will be evaluated.

Number One – Unity, Independence, and Supremacy

The number one has three distinct meanings in Scripture, all of which are essential to God: He is *unified*, while being *independent* and *supreme* over all things. Quoting Deuteronomy 6:4, the Lord Jesus affirmed that *"the Lord our God is one Lord."* The Hebrew word for God in Deuteronomy 6:4 is *Elohim*, a plural noun for God. The Hebrew word rendered "one" is *echad*, meaning "united with" or "one of others," to signify a compound unity – the Trinity (i.e., three in one and one in three). This means that there is only one God and He exists in plural persons as Lord of all. The meaning of *echad* appears again in Genesis 2:24 to explain how a husband and a wife become *one* flesh (a compound unity) through marriage; *"the two become one."* This explains why the Hebrew word *yacheed (yachiyd)*, which means "only one," is never used to describe God. *Yacheed* is used by God to indicate that Isaac was Abraham's *only* son of promise (Genesis 22:2, 12, 16).

In foretelling of Christ's return to the Earth to establish His kingdom, the prophet Zechariah wrote: *"The Lord shall be King over all the Earth. In that day it shall be – 'the Lord is one' and His name one"* (Zech. 14:9). There is only one Lord and there shall never be another and He exists in perfect unity – oneness. This is why the Lord Jesus could declare, *"I and My Father are one"* (John 10:30).

But not only does God exist in unity as one, but one is also the chief ordinal pertaining to God; He is the "First." He is supreme over everything. Speaking of Himself, the Lord Jesus told John, *"I am the First and the Last"* (Rev. 1:17). Here, "First" is a divine title. The Lord as the Great I Am is eternally self-existing and has authority over all things. He is the Creator and the source of all life; He is the First!

In becoming one with Christ through spiritual rebirth, we share in the blessedness of God's unity, independence, and supremacy over His creation (1 Cor. 10:16-17; Eph. 4:4-6). The Lord Jesus highlights this reality while addressing His Father in prayer the night before His crucifixion:

> *And the glory which You gave Me I have given them, that they may be one just as We are one: I in them, and You in Me; that they may be made perfect in one, and that the world may know that You have sent Me, and have loved them as You have loved Me* (John 17:22–23).

While unity, independence, and supremacy are essential to who God is, believers are blessed by these attributes through their oneness with God in Christ. While the number *one* primarily pertains to God, we do find these same ideas conveyed in lower applications within Scripture, especially the concept of unity. For example, when a man and a woman are joined through a marriage covenant, the two become "one flesh" (Gen. 2:24). Also, while speaking to Pharaoh about his two recurring dreams, Joseph said: *"The dreams of Pharaoh are one* [one with each other]*; God has shown Pharaoh what He is about to do"* (Gen. 41:25). Both dreams were one, thus indicating that they were unified in meaning.

Two – Difference, Union, and Testimony

The number *two* plainly contrasts the number *one* in meaning. Where the number *one* excludes the possibility of difference, the number *two* affirms it. *One* speaks of unity, but *two* speaks of division and distinction. *Two* is the first number that divides evenly and therefore it often represents animosity and conflict, which may be morally good or for evil. An example of this divisive tenor is contained within the Lord's teaching about commitment: *"No one can serve two masters; for either he will hate the one and love the other, or else he will be loyal to the one and despise the other. You cannot serve God and mammon"* (Matt. 6:24). No one can serve the Lord, as he or she should, if suffering from a divided heart. In this application, the number *two* is used in a negative sense to warn against half-hearted commitment to the Lord.

However, Solomon highlights a positive side of the number *two* – the benefit of *union*:

> *Two are better than one, because they have a good reward for their labor. For if they fall, one will lift up his companion. But woe to him who is alone when he falls, for he has no one to help him up. Again, if two lie down together, they will keep warm; but how can one be warm alone? Though one may be overpowered by another, two can withstand him* (Eccles. 4:9-12).

The idea is that although the number *two* calls our attention to distinction, two different things binding together in oneness are stronger than either part separately. So, when used in the good sense, the number *two* speaks of the act of unifying – *union*.

A third way in which the number *two* is employed in Scripture is to speak of the reliable testimony of *two witnesses*. The Lord Jesus affirmed this fact to the Pharisees who were challenging the validity of His testimony: *"It is also written in your law that the testimony of two men is true"* (John 8:17). The Lord practiced this idea in that when He sent His disciples throughout Galilee and later Judea to preach the Kingdom message to His countrymen, He sent the disciples out "two by two" (Luke 10:1). There would be greater safety for those sharing the gospel as they went out in pairs and there would be a stronger testimony of the truth affirmed by *two* witnesses rather than one.

Three – Completeness, Perfection, and Resurrection

The number *three* is the first of four numbers which represent various forms of *completion* and *perfection* in Scripture; *seven*, *ten*, and *twelve* are the other three. God is triune, the Father, the Son, and the Holy Spirit (Matt. 28:19; 1 Cor. 8:6; 2 Cor. 13:14); hence, *three* denotes the fullness, completeness, and divine perfection of the Godhead (Col. 2:9). God the

Father spoke from heaven three times to express His full delight and appreciation for the completeness of His Son's earthly ministry.

We are three-dimensional beings that exist in a three-dimensional world. We naturally connect height, width, and depth to what is solid; that is what is real and substantial to us. This is the idea attached to the number *three*. Obviously, God, being *three in one,* is real, substantial, and perfectly complete.

The number *three* is also used in a special way to remind us of resurrection. Speaking of His death, the Lord said that He would *"be raised the third day"* after being crucified (Matt. 16:21, 17:23, 20:19). The Lord offered His resurrection as a sign to the Pharisees that would prove His credentials as the Son of God. He refers to this as the sign of Jonah, who was in the belly of a great fish three days before being vomited out on dry land. Moreover, Mark records that the Lord Jesus was crucified at the "third hour" (or 9:00 A.M.; Mark 15:25).

Interestingly, there are three resurrections recorded in the Old Testament, and then Christ performed three more during His earthly ministry, before affecting His own resurrection, the *seventh* in Scripture, the *perfect* resurrection.

Genesis 22 records the first time that resurrection is alluded to in the Old Testament. It took Abraham three days to reach Moriah, the appointed sacrificial site where God had commanded Abraham to offer Isaac, his beloved son. Why did the journey require three days and not two or four? Because in Abraham's mind, God's will and command could not be thwarted; thus, Isaac was as good as dead for those three days – this duration prophetically typifies the three days between the Lord Jesus' death and resurrection. After arriving at Moriah, he instructed the two young men with him to wait at the base of the mountain while he and Isaac offered a sacrifice, then he *and Isaac* would return to them. How did Abraham know that Isaac would return with him? We get a clue from Hebrews 11:17-19. Abraham by faith knew that Isaac was the promised seed and that God could not breach His word – so if he struck Isaac down, God would have to raise him back to life.

The number *three* is present in each of the three Old Testament accounts of resurrection. Elijah stretched himself over the widow of Zarephath's deceased son three times before he revived (1 Kgs. 17:21). Then Elisha raised the deceased son of the Shunammite woman by putting his mouth on the child's mouth, his eyes on the child's eyes, and his hands on the child's hands (2 Kgs. 4:34). The third and, by design, last resurrection of the Old Testament occurred when some men hastily cast the body of a man in the sepulcher of Elisha to escape from the invading Moabites; the man immediately revived.

Four – Earthly Order

The number *four* is used to symbolize earthly order, as created by God. Here are a few expressions of this use of the number *four* in Scripture. There are…

> *Four* seasons (Spring, Summer, Fall, and Winter).
> *Four* regions/directions (North, South, East, and West).
> *Four* divisions of day (morning, noon, evening, and night).
> *Four* phases of the moon (new, half waxing, full, half waning).
> *Four* winds (from the four directions previously mentioned).
> *Four* realms in which creatures dwell (on the ground, under the ground, in the sky, or in the sea).
> *Four* means of dividing the human race (kindred, people, tongue, and nation).
> *Four* types of soils to reflect the hearts of men (hard, stony, thorny, and good unto fruitfulness).

There are many instances in which *earthly order* is symbolized by the number *four* in Scripture. For example, after God rested from His six days of creation work, we read that *"a river went out of Eden to water the garden, and from there it parted and became four riverheads"* (Gen. 2:10). Each river went a different direction to refresh the entire land, symbolizing that the whole world was receiving the blessing of God's presence and rest.

A second example of the number *four* being used to signify the earthly domain is in how it is incorporated into the design of the tabernacle, as recorded by Moses in the book of Exodus. The ceiling tapestry, referred to as the tabernacle, was composed of four different colored threads which were woven together. Three more coverings were placed upon it to make a total of four layers over the tabernacle walls. The inner veil hung on four pillars (Ex. 26:31-32), forming a barrier between the Most Holy Place where God dwelt and the Holy Place where the priests entered twice daily. Like the ceiling tapestry, the veil was woven of the same four colors and it also displayed the figures of cherubim (note that cherubim have four wings and four faces). Moving into the Holy Place, we notice that the Golden Altar of Incense has four horns extending up from itself. The holy ointment, which was dabbed on parts of the tabernacle, and the prepared incense, which was placed twice daily upon the Golden Altar, were each composed of four spices.

Venturing eastward through the Holy Place into the courtyard, four more horns are noted upon the Bronze Altar. Beyond the Bronze Altar, the only entrance to the tabernacle courtyard is seen; it is formed by "hangings" upon four pillars. Like the tabernacle coverings and the inner veil, the "hangings" were also woven from four differently colored threads. Lastly, we notice that the priests offer only four types of creatures upon the Bronze Altar: the bullock, the lamb, the goat, and the turtledove. The number *four* pervades the journey from God's presence to man's realm of life – it is the same path the Son of God traveled to become the Son of Man to fulfill His earthly ministry.

A third example of the symbolic meaning of the number *four* is offered in how God chose to reveal His Son to humanity. Have you ever wondered why God chose to reveal His Son to us through four gospel accounts? Why not use *seven*, the number of perfection, to present His Son to the world instead of *four*? The reason is that the number *four* better represents what the Son of God did by coming into the world than the number *seven*. When the Son exited the dimensionless and timeless realm of majesty on high and descended to the Earth, He willingly placed Himself under earthly order. As a man, He became subject to the natural laws of creation, even though, as God, He still maintained the order of all things (Col. 1:17). Consequently, the Lord never allowed His deity to satisfy His humanity beyond the normal scope in which all humanity experiences the daily blessings of God.

In becoming the Son of Man, God is not emphasizing His Son's deity, but rather His lowly position and ministry on the Earth. The Spirit of God, throughout the Bible, consistently represents the glories of the Son, while being *earthly-connected*, by employing the number *four*.

Accordingly, the four Gospels uphold the brilliancy of the Lord both from a different perspective and to a unique earthly audience. Matthew presents Christ to a Jewish audience as the legitimate King to the throne of David. Writing to a Roman audience, Mark speaks of the lowly Servant of Jehovah. Luke upholds Christ's perfect humanity to the Greeks. John proclaims the deity of Christ to the whole world.

The Father provided perfect representation of His Son through these four unique vantage points of His greatness. *Four* is the number pertaining to *earthly order*. It is the best number to declare the "good news" message – that the Son of God willingly departed heaven to live on a sin-cursed planet for the purpose of suffering and dying for the good of others. The Gospel of Jesus Christ, from every viewpoint, is "good news" indeed!

It is observed that the number *four* is the first number that is divisible ($4 \div 2 = 2$). But as previously noted, God rarely *divides* four in this way to reveal divine mysteries in Scripture; He normally combines the numbers *one* and *three* to create four. By devising a *three-and-one* Gospel format (the Synoptic Gospels and John), God has upheld the symbolic scriptural meanings of the numbers *one* and *three* to represent His Son to the world. Number *one* represents divine unity and speaks of the Creator, while the number *three* signifies divine fullness and perfection.

A fourth example of the number *four's* metaphoric meaning is found in Revelation 7:1, which reads: *"After these things I saw four angels standing at the four corners of the earth, holding the four winds of the earth, that the wind should not blow on the earth, on the sea, or on any tree."* Some skeptics have pointed to the *"four corners of the earth"* statement of this verse as evidence that the Bible declares that the planet Earth has corners. The Greek word translated "corners" is *gonia* and is understood to mean a literal "corner" or regional "quarters."

Most revelation in the prophetic books of the Bible was given audibly, but we understand that the means of conveying information in Revelation would be mainly through viewed symbols and figurative scenes (Rev. 1:1). Thus, the reference to "the four quarters of the earth" simply implies an immediate worldwide cessation of judgment so that the 144,000 Jewish witnesses can be safely sealed (Rev. 7:2-8). The number *four* is being symbolically employed in this verse to speak of God's complete control over the Earth to accomplish His purposes.

Five – Divine Grace and Goodness

As previously mentioned, the number *five* is usually obtained by combining the numbers *one* and *four* together. *One* speaks of our all-sufficient God, while *four* declares His creative work as pertaining to man (i.e., earthly order). Through the all-sufficient God's redemptive work, He is able to offer *grace* to man, though humanity corrupted His creative work by sin in Eden. In the *five* books of the Law, God reveals man's failure (Genesis) and His remedy, substitutional death of a perfect sacrifice for the guilty (Exodus-Deuteronomy).

What is the first thing that new parents do when they see their newborn for the first time? They often will count all the baby's toes and fingers to verify the healthiness of their child. *Five* fingers on each hand and *five* toes on each foot was a cursory check to establish the healthiness of the baby. In grace, God bestowed man *five* senses (sight, hearing, taste, smell, and touch) to appreciate His blessings from God.

Israel would continue experiencing the grace and goodness of God, if they presented the *five* Levitical offerings (the burnt, the meal, the peace, the sin and the trespass offerings). The holy anointing oil to be used to consecrate the tabernacle, its articles, and the priests and their attire was a mixture of *five* ingredients: olive oil and four spices – myrrh, cinnamon, sweet-smelling cane (calamus), and cassia (Ex. 30:23-31).

The number *five* was prominent in the tabernacle, which permitted God to dwell among men and to experience His goodness. The assembled board walls on three sides were to be reinforced by *five* bars (Ex. 26:26-28). The entrance of the tabernacle was composed of *five* pillars and sockets (Ex. 26:27). The Bronze Altar for atoning sacrifices was *five* cubits long and *five* cubits wide (Ex. 27:1). The curtain wall encircling the tabernacle to create its courtyard was *five* cubits high (Ex. 27:18).

The Church would experience the goodness of Christ through *five* special gifts given to edify the Church: apostles, prophets, evangelists, teachers, and shepherds (Eph. 4:11-12).

David chose *five* smooth stones from the brook before facing the giant Goliath in battle (1 Sam. 17:40). By God's grace, David would not only defeat Goliath, but he and his mighty men would slay his four giant brothers also.

There are also *five* women listed in the genealogy of Christ (Matt. 1) that were of poor reputation, socially speaking, but experienced God's grace in wonderful ways. There are several passages of Scripture that specifically mention the word "grace" only five times (e.g., Ex. 33:12-17; Rom. 5:15-21, 11:5-6; 2 Cor. 8).

God would demonstrate His fathomless grace to humanity by sending His own Son into the world on their behalf. Accordingly, Isaiah refers to Messiah's name by ascribing Him *five* titles: Wonderful,

Counselor, the Mighty God, the Everlasting Father, and the Prince of Peace (Isa. 9:6).

We only find the Greek word *parakleetos* used five times in the New Testament. In John's gospel, the Lord used *parakleetos* four times to foretell to His disciples of their forthcoming *Helper* and *Comforter*, speaking of the Holy Spirit (see John 14:12-16). John later translates *parakleetos* as *Advocate* to speak of Christ's ongoing representation of all believers before God's throne in heaven (1 Jn. 2:1). These are *five* lovely expressions of God's grace to all believers.

Lastly, there are several occurrences in Scripture in which the *fifth* mention of a specific Bible character's name is accompanied by the word "grace" (or "favor"): Noah (6:8), Boaz (Ruth 1:8-10), Ruth (Ruth 2:2), and David (1 Sam. 16:22).

Six – Man's Weakness and Sin, Satan's Evil

Six is the product of *two* and *three*. The number *two* symbolizes division or testimony and the number *three* represents fullness or completion. Combining these two aspects infers that the number *six* pictures the full weakness of man separated from God and the complete manifestation of evil. The number *six* then has two meanings.

First, it symbolizes man's weakness or limitations. Man was created on the *sixth* day of creation (Gen. 1:24-31) and was to labor on *six* days of the week before resting on the seventh (Ex. 9:10). A Jewish man or woman was not to be a slave in Israel for more than *six* years (Ex. 21:2). Moses waited *six* days on Mount Sinai before God revealed Himself to him (Ex. 24:15-18). Solomon's wisdom and vast kingdom was magnificent. He built an elaborate ivory throne with *six* steps to rule from (1 Kgs. 10:19). But *six* is one short of *seven*, the number of perfection, and Solomon's deficiencies became evident after committing idolatry in the latter years of his reign. The number *six* refers to God's restraint over humanity's vitality and will, the former, governed by the latter, naturally resists God's control.

Second, the number *six* refers to the manifestation of evil. In the opening pages of Genesis, we are introduced to a Triune God who identifies Himself by plural nouns and pronouns, then Adam, then the woman (later named Eve), and then the serpent. Hence, Satan is the sixth character revealed to us in Scripture, which illustrates his negative influence – he is on the opposite side of man, in respect to God, so to speak.

This mystery of lawlessness reaches its apex during the Tribulation Period and is thus represented in the number *666*. This is the number associated with the mark of the beast during *The Time of Jacob's Trouble* (Rev. 13:18). It is the number associated with the complete manifestation of evil, *six*, that is repeated 3 times to indicate its utter climax. The greatest opposition of humanity to God's rule will be the most evident during this seven-year period, as the Antichrist rules over the world.

Seven – Spiritual Perfection and Completeness

Being a prime number, *seven* cannot be subjected to true division. As noted earlier, the division of *seven* in Scripture is almost always into *three* and *four* to indicate that divine manifestation is occurring in the world order. *Seven* is the second of four numbers used to symbolize perfection (*three*, *ten*, and *twelve* are the others), but the number *seven* is especially connected to God personally – it is God's number.

God manifests His character and attributes to humanity by what He does. Hence, *seven* is the number of *divine perfection* as demonstrated in God's accomplishments. This is why Noah waited *seven* days in the ark before the flood came (Gen. 7:9-10), and why Aaron and his sons had to complete a *seven*-day sanctifying process to be consecrated as holy priests in the Lord's presence (Lev. 8:31-36), and why the blood on the Day of Atonement had to be sprinkled on and before the Mercy Seat seven times (Lev. 16:14). In the Law given to Israel, God sanctified the *seventh* day, the *seventh* year, and the year following the *forty-ninth* year (i.e., 7 x 7th year) – the year of Jubilee (Lev. 25:8-12). By observing the number *seven* in this way, man is acknowledging God is perfect and all His ways are perfect too.

The number *seven* is identified as God's number of perfection and completeness in the first chapter of the Bible. In the creation account of Genesis 1, we read *seven* times *"and God said,"* and then *seven* times of what God thought of what He had accomplished, *"it was good."* God was completely satisfied with all that He had done.

Interestingly, the *seventh* time Noah's name appears in Scripture, we read: *"Noah was a just man, perfect in his generations"* (Gen. 6:9). Enoch, Noah's great-grandfather, was a man who walked with God; he was the *seventh* generation in Adam's line through Seth (Gen. 5).

The Hebrew text of Genesis 1:1 declares that God's work in creation was perfect. The verse is composed of *seven* Hebrew words and contains *twenty-eight* letters. As already mentioned, the number *four* is the number for creation or the created world. In the Hebrew language, this statement is made up of seven Hebrew words, comprising twenty-eight letters. The text states literally, *"In the beginning God created the heavens and the Earth"* and metaphorically, by utilizing the numbers *four* and *seven*, it is declared a perfect creation.

The book of Revelation, the apocalypse of Jesus Christ, is saturated with the number *seven* to highlight the perfect manifestation of Christ's authority and righteousness in all His judgments. There are seven: churches, Spirits (speaking of the perfection of the Holy Spirit), stars, seal judgments, trumpet judgments, bowl judgments, dooms, and new things. In the NKJV of the Bible, the words "seven," "seventh," "sevenfold," and "sevens" are found 568 times and 65 of those are in the book of Revelation.

The Gospel of John upholds the divine perfections of the Lord Jesus Christ; hence, it is no surprise that the number *seven* permeates John's record. There are ...

Seven discourses: The New Birth (3:1-36), The Water of Life (4:1-42), The Divine Son (5:19-47), The Bread of Life (6:22-66), The Life-Giving Spirit (7:1-52), The Light of the World (8:12-59), and The Good Shepherd (10:1-42).

Seven feasts or holy convocations: First Passover (2:13, 23), Feast of the Jews – Second Passover (5:1), Third Passover (6:4), Tabernacles (7:2), The Great Day of Convocation (7:37; Lev. 23:36), Dedication (10:22), and Fourth Passover (11:55).

Seven witnesses of Christ's deity: John the Baptizer (1:29-34), Nathaniel (1:43-51), Peter (6:66-69), the Lord Jesus (10:22-30), Martha (11:27), Thomas (20:28), and John (1:14, 20:30-31).

Seven times Christ instructed His disciples to pray in His name.

Seven times the word "hate" is found in John 15.

Seven ministries of the Holy Spirit to the believer are noted (John 16).

Seven times Christ referred to believers as the Father's "gift" to Him (John 17).

Seven times John recorded that Christ spoke only the Word of the Father.

Seven times the writer of John (John) referred to himself but not by name.

Seven important events pertaining to Christ's ministry appear in all four Gospels: The ministry of John the Baptist as the forerunner of Christ, the feeding of the 5000, Peter's confession of Jesus being the Christ, the Triumphal Entry presentation of Messiah, and the crucifixion, burial and resurrection of the Lord.

Eight – New Beginnings

The number *eight* is repeatedly used to speak of *new beginnings*, such as new life (e.g., regeneration or resurrection) or a new order of things. In actuality, we are already familiar with this concept: the *eighth* day begins a new week in our calendars and the *eighth* note in a musical scale begins a new octave. *Seven* is God's number of completeness (Gen. 2:3), which means *eight* is the start of a new series, just as the *seventh* day, Saturday, yields to the *eighth*, Sunday, to begin a new week. Accordingly, the Lord arose from the tomb on Sunday to demonstrate the newness of His resurrection life.

This symbolism can be seen throughout both the Pentateuch and the history books of the Old Testament. The *eighth* time that Noah's name is mentioned in Genesis, we read *"Noah walked with God"* (Gen. 6:9). This was a new way of life for Noah and for us too. A few years later, Noah and his family, *eight* souls, entered an ark (a picture of Christ), to escape God's judgment upon the wicked through a flood (Gen. 7:7; 1 Pet. 3:20). The ark protected its occupants from God's wrath, lifted them off the Earth to be alone with God, and safely carried them to a new life in a new world. Abraham was commanded to circumcise the newborn males of his household on the *eighth* day, symbolizing the consecration of a new life to God (Gen. 17:12).

As Leviticus introduces a new era of opportunity for the Jewish nation to *come near* to Jehovah, the word *"eighth"* appears ten times, significantly more than any other book in the Bible. It fact, one-fourth of all occurrences of the word "eighth" in the Bible are found in Leviticus. While Genesis is a book of initial "beginnings," Leviticus (which institutes blood atonement and blood cleansing) is a continuing story of "new beginnings" after the fall of mankind. The Levitical priests began their service to the Lord in the tabernacle on the *eighth* day (after seven days of purification and consecration had been completed; Lev. 8:31-36).

Under the Law, Jewish males were circumcised on the eighth day after birth to symbolize identification with God's covenant, but in the Age of Grace, circumcision of the heart is what is stressed. This represented living in a new way and having a consecrated life to God through the power of the Holy Spirit (Rom. 8:2:28-29; Col. 2:11-13).

The prophet Samuel was to anoint a new king of Israel, a man after God's own heart – that man was David, the *eighth* son of Jesse (1 Sam. 17:12). Through David, a new and everlasting dynasty would be established: the Lord Jesus Christ will rule from the throne of David forever.

A curious Pharisee named Nicodemus secretly visited the Lord Jesus one night. The Lord told him that he could not enter heaven without being born again (John 3:3). In this discussion the word "born" occurs *eight* times to speak of a new beginning with God through spiritual rebirth (John 3:1-8). While talking with a Samaritan woman at Jacob's well, the Lord Jesus invites her to drink of Himself, so that her soul will never be thirsty again. During this dialogue, the word "water" occurs *eight* times (John 4:4-15). She did drink of Him that very day and experienced a new beginning with God.

Nine – Finality and Spiritual Fruitfulness

The number *nine* is the last of the single-digit numerals and thus speaks of finality. Numbers beyond *nine* are merely composed of the first ten digits (i.e., whole numbers *zero* to *nine*). The number *nine* is the product of *three* times *three*. Three, symbolizing completeness and perfection, is the first of four perfect numbers. The number *nine* then expresses *finality*; God makes the believer complete through spiritual regeneration. The indwelling Holy Spirit enables the believer to serve Christ and to enjoy perfect oneness with Him. Although fellowship with God is hindered by sin, our blessed union with Him is final – forever!

After suffering on the cross for six hours, the Lord Jesus concluded His work of propitiation for us on the *ninth* hour (Matt. 27:45-50). Before commending His spirit to His Father, the Lord cried out with a loud voice, *"It is finished"* (John 19:30). The Lord's declaration of finality is tied with the number *nine*.

According to the Law, the method of judicial execution (to end the life of a Law-breaker) was to be by public stoning. Yet, the whole of Scripture only records nine instances of a public stoning: the blasphemer (Lev. 24:16), the Sabbath-breaker (Num. 15:36), Achan (Josh. 7:25), Abimelech (Judg. 9:53), Adoram (1 Kgs. 12:18), Naboth (1 Kgs 21:10), Zechariah (2 Chron. 24:21), Stephen (Acts 7:59), and Paul at Lystra (Acts 14:19). The crowd that stoned Paul assumed that he was dead, but afterwards He suddenly stood up unharmed. Paul had either experienced bodily resurrection or he had been miraculously healed from his injuries.

Nine follows the number *eight*, just as spiritual fruitfulness is to naturally follow a believer's spiritual birth in Christ. On several occasions, the Lord Jesus told His disciples that only good trees bear good fruit, and, likewise, that bad trees produce according to their nature (Matt. 7:17). His point was that a true believer is known by his or her fruit in the same way that *"a tree is known by its fruit"* (Matt. 12:33). Apple trees do not produce pears; they bear only apples. This means that true Christians will be characterized by the fruit of the Spirit, not by works of the flesh.

Paul informs us that there are nine qualities to *the fruit of the Spirit*: *"The fruit of the Spirit is love, joy, peace, longsuffering, kindness, goodness, faithfulness, gentleness, self-control. Against such there is no law"* (Gal. 5:22-23). Paul refers to "the fruit of the Spirit," not "the fruits of the Spirit." The fruit of the Spirit is homogenous in expressing the character of God in the believer's behavior, thus "fruit" and not "fruits." The qualities of this fruit relate to three categories of associations: Love, joy, and peace pertain to our union with Christ. Longsuffering, gentleness, and goodness relate to our interaction with others. Faithfulness, meekness, and self-control are in relationship to self.

The Holy Spirit longs for us to experience the love, joy, and peace of Christ in our lives; these *nine* eternal qualities are only found in God. The Holy Spirit also enables us to be patient, kind, gentle, longsuffering, forgiving in our interactions with others; we want to show others the goodness of God that we ourselves are experiencing. The Holy Spirit also wants us to be full of faith, and to keep our carnal nature in check. All that we do and say should be guided by meekness and self-control.

The work of the Holy Spirit in the lives of believers is again evident in the giving of spiritual gifts (1 Cor. 12:8-10). Although there are many other spirituals gifts bestowed to the Church and believers, Paul lists *nine* gifts in this passage.

Ten – Divine Order and Responsibility

The number *ten* begins a new series of numbers (ten through nineteen). In Scripture, the number *ten* denotes *the perfection of God's revealed order*. Through Moses and Aaron, God provided a powerful testimony of Himself throughout Egypt; this is why there are *ten* specific plagues and not *nine* or *eleven*. The Exodus narrative reveals that Pharaoh hardened his own heart *ten* times against God's command to liberate His people. Pharaoh was accountable to God, who was in full control of the situation; hence, the text also records that God hardened Pharaoh's heart on *ten* specific occasions to accomplish His sovereign purposes. The number *ten* is repetitively used in Scripture to signify a *divine testimony* that results in human responsibility. The *ten* plagues announced by Moses on God's behalf would provide an awesome testimony of God's power and righteousness, and at the same time, put the Egyptians under personal accountability to Him.

Similarly, *ten* was used to reveal God's Law to the Israelites and to affix their immediate accountability to it (Ex. 20). The Ten Commandments represent God's standard of righteousness; the Jews would be blessed for obedience and judged for waywardness. The number *ten* is then used extensively in the tabernacle's dimensions and features to again convey the idea of God's testimony among His people and their responsibility to obey His ordained system of worship. Accordingly, God demanded that His covenant people return to Him a *tithe* (a *tenth*) of what they had received from Him; their response would be a testimony of their trust in the Lord and also His faithfulness to them (Mal. 3:10).

Ten is the sum of *four* and *six*. As already mentioned, the number *four* represents *earthly order*, while the number *six* pertains to man. Just as *six* falls short of *seven* (the perfect number), man falls short of God's glory (Rom. 3:23). The combination of these numbers then represents man's accountability to God's revealed order.

The *ten* virgins waiting for the Bridegroom affirms their responsibility to be watching and waiting for Him (Matt. 25:1-13); however, five virgins did not take the matter seriously and were later excluded from attending the wedding. *Ten* servants are each given a mina to invest for their master during his long journey; each servant had to give an account of their stewardship when he returned (Luke 19:12-27).

Eleven – Judgment and Disorder

The number *eleven* (including *eleventh*) appears only forty-four times in the entire Bible and is mostly used in a literal sense. This means that determining the number's metaphoric meaning is more challenging. The number *ten* represents God's testimony, which man is accountable to obey. *Eleven* being one more than *ten* calls our attention to the consequences of disregarding God's law – *judgment* follows disobedience. *Eleven* is also one less than *twelve*, which represents *divine government*. Fallible human governments fall short of God's perfect rulership. The number *eleven* seems to affirm that divine judgment follows willful rebellion of what God condones and that inevitably man falls short of reflecting God's perfect character in what he does.

An example of this idea is when God revealed His Law to the Israelites at Mount Sinai (also called Mount Horeb), but then led them to Kadesh Barnea, so that they could enter into the Promised Land and seize their inheritance. This journey took *eleven* days (Deut. 1:2). God's Law (the number *ten*) was on one side of their journey, and a new home/order in which God would rule over His people on the other side (the number *twelve*). But after listening to the report of ten Jewish spies, the people rebelled against the Lord at Kadesh Barnea and would not enter Canaan. God therefore punished all those twenty years old and older (excluding Joshua and Caleb); they would never see Canaan, but would rather wander and perish in the wilderness during the next thirty-eight-plus years (Num. 13-14).

Interestingly, Scripture records *eleven* times that particular individuals in authority were offended when God's word was revealed to them: Pharaoh, King Balak of Moab, Kings Jeroboam and Ahab of Israel, Kings Asa, Joash, Uzziah, Jehoiakim, and Zedekiah of Judah, Naaman (a captain in the Syrian army), and Herod Antipas. Except for Naaman, who judged his own pride and experienced God's grace, varying degrees of God's judgment fell on the remaining individuals.

Because Pharaoh would not release the Israelites as Jehovah commanded, Moses and Aaron announced ten plagues on Egypt to liberate them. The tenth plague, the death of the firstborn, was used to reveal God's provision of redemption through the blood of the Passover lamb, which was available to anyone who wanted to be saved from God's wrath. This provision, however, was not forced; only those wanting salvation would apply the blood to the doorframe of their homes. But this is not the end of the story; there was one more judgment on Egypt to secure those delivered from Egypt by the blood of the Passover lamb.

Pharaoh's army was completely wiped out in the Red Sea, which brought complete deliverance to the Israelites (Ex. 14). By the *eleventh* judgment, God completely secured what He had already redeemed and sanctified for Himself and also judged those who ignored the testimony of His ten previous plagues.

Noah pronounced judgment on Ham's son, Canaan, after his son Ham disrespected him (Gen. 9:20-25). We learn in Genesis 10 that Canaan had *eleven* sons, which seems to show God's endorsement of Noah's curse placed on Ham.

The last king of the Southern Kingdom of Judah was a wicked man named Zedekiah. He rebelled against God's commandment to surrender Jerusalem to Babylon, as delivered through the prophet Jeremiah. We read that Babylon besieged the city and that he was eventually captured, blinded, and carried away to Babylon where he died (Jer. 52:1-9). Judgment fell on Zedekiah in the *eleventh* year of his reign.

As a young man, Joseph revealed two prophetic dreams to his ten older brothers, which indicated that they (including his younger brother Benjamin) would all bow down to him in a coming day (Gen. 37:5-11). Joseph's ten older brothers rejected the idea of him ruling over them and therefore sold him into slavery (Gen. 37:28). When Joseph was nearly forty, the dreams were fulfilled, as He had become second-ruler over Egypt and his brethren willingly honored his authority (Gen. 45). The narrative connects the numbers *ten* and *eleven* together: *ten* rejected God's revealed will and *eleven* experienced the humiliating aftermath of that decision.

Similarly, there were *twelve* disciples chosen by the Lord Jesus, but one rejected the truth and fell into judgment, leaving *eleven* (Luke 24:9, 33). In a lessor sense, *eleven* may also represent *incompleteness* or *disorder*, as the eleven disciples did not feel that they were complete until a replacement disciple had been recognized (Acts 1:20-26). The Lord felt the same way about the matter and chose Paul as the *twelfth* disciple; thus, His governing authority in the Church is represented by the *twelve* apostles throughout eternity (Rev. 21:14).

Twelve is the number of governmental perfection (God's order to be heeded), while *ten* is the number of divine testimony (His law to be obeyed). Like *three* and *seven*, *ten* and *twelve* are perfect numbers (i.e., each number pertains to God). *Eleven* is between *ten* and *twelve* any time man fails to obey God's law or order, there will be painful consequences.

Twelve – Governmental Perfection

The number *twelve* indicates completeness of a government or administration, usually divinely appointed. In the Old Testament, the number *twelve* is often used as the signature of the nation of Israel (*twelve* tribes, though there were actually thirteen tribes). In the New Testament, *twelve* is used to show the complete administration of the Church (*twelve* apostles).

This representation of Church authority will be recognized during the Kingdom Age. The Lord Jesus promised that when He returned to the Earth to establish His kingdom, the *twelve* apostles would sit on *twelve* thrones and rule over the *twelve* tribes of Israel (Matt. 19:28). Hence, the number *twelve* is used in Scripture to express God's governmental authority during the era of the Law, the Church Age, and the Kingdom Age.

The twelve tribes of Israel are repeatedly represented in type throughout the Old Testament in various ways, such as in the number of stones in the High Priest's breastplate and the number of unleavened loaves on the Table of Showbread, and in Elijah's altar of twelve stones on Mount Carmel. This depiction of Israel continues in the New Testament, as the woman in Revelation 12 is wearing a crown of twelve stars and the New Jerusalem described in Revelation 21 has twelve gates, representing each tribe of Israel. The New Jerusalem has twelve foundations, one for each of the twelve apostles from the Church Age also. Both Jew and Gentile will be blessed by God's perfect governmental authority forever.

God established the Hebrew calendar; there were to be twelve months in a calendar year; this represented God's governing order of time for all those dwelling on the Earth.

The compounded meaning of the numbers *four* and *three* is shown in the meanings of *seven* and *twelve*. *Three* (picturing *divine perfection*) and *four* (symbolizing *earthly order*) are added to make *seven*, thus showing God's complete control of His creation. The product of *three* and *four* is *twelve*, which brings this idea to its apex – God declares His sovereign rule over His creation. *Twelve* signifies God's *governmental perfection over* what is His, while *ten* represents *perfect order for* what is His.

Thirteen – Rebellion and Depravity

We find the first mention of the number *thirteen* in Genesis 14. The cities of the Jordan plain, where Lot lived, had been in servitude to an Eastern king named Chedorlaomer for twelve years. The five Jordanian kings rebelled in the *thirteenth* year. The following year, Chedorlaomer came with three other kings from the east (Tidal, Amraphel, and Arioch) to recompense the Jordanians for their insurrection.

The next significant usage of the number *thirteen* is observed in God's response to Abram after his lapse of faith in taking Hagar as a concubine to raise up children for Sarai, instead of waiting on God to fulfill his promise that Abram and Sarai would have a son (Gen. 16). God waited *thirteen* years before confronting Abram's disobedience and then reminded Abram of His "covenant" *thirteen* times (Gen. 17). Apparently, the Lord was addressing Abram's past lapse of faith through the meaning of the number *thirteen*, in the same way that the Lord Jesus reproved Peter in John 21. Peter had publicly denied the Lord three times, and the Lord also inquired of Peter three times concerning his love for Him (John 21).

Other occurrences of the number *thirteen* symbolizing rebellion in Scripture include: Haman's decree to kill the Jews, God's chosen people, on the *thirteenth* day of the twelfth month (Est. 3:8-13). *Thirteen* judges are recorded ruling over Israel during a time when everyone did what was right in their own eyes (Judg. 17:6). The prophet Jeremiah delivered *thirteen* messages to treacherous Judah, whom he calls a *backsliding* people *thirteen* times. Jeremiah's prophetic ministry began in the *thirteenth* year of King Josiah's reign. The Israelites marched around rebellious Jericho *thirteen* times before God destroyed the city (Josh. 7). As God instructed His people not to observe the Sabbath Day to accomplish this feat, the significance of *thirteen* encirclements in *seven* days is significant.

God lists twenty-three grievances in Romans 1:29-31 against fallen humanity, and the *thirteenth* is "haters of God." Of course, the greatest "hater of God" would be Satan himself; thus, he is referred to *thirteen*

Bible Numbers and Symbols

times in the book of Revelation as the "dragon." The first man to instigate mass rebellion against God on the Earth was a man named Nimrod, who was the father of pagan Babylonian religion. Nimrod was the *thirteenth* in the cursed line of Ham (Noah's youngest son). Lastly, the Lord used a total of *thirteen* evil characteristics in Mark 7:21-22 to describe a depraved and rebellious heart.

Fourteen – Deliverance and Salvation

The number *fourteen* (including *fourteenth*) is found 49 times in the Bible; its first significant metaphoric use is found in Exodus 12 and 13. The Passover lambs were slaughtered and their blood was applied on the door frames of each house where those within desired to be spared from God's judgment of the firstborn throughout Egypt. By faith, the applied blood of the lamb also brought *deliverance* from Egypt and slavery to that household. It is the same for those who apply, by faith, the blood of Christ's sacrifice to their own souls – they experience a deliverance from Egypt (worldliness) and from bondage (being enslaved to sin).

God's Passover Lamb for humanity is first introduced to us in the New Testament by Matthew's detailed genealogy (Matt. 1). The apostle is proving to his Jewish audience that Christ is a descendant of Abraham through David and thus a legitimate heir to David's throne forever. Interestingly, Matthew purposely skips a generation here and there to provide a symbolic representation of the number *fourteen* in the order of Christ's genealogy:

> *So all the generations from Abraham to David are fourteen generations, from David until the captivity in Babylon are fourteen generations, and from the captivity in Babylon until the Christ are fourteen generations* (Matt. 1:17).

Why did Matthew carefully order Christ's genealogy around the number *fourteen*? Louis Barbieri explains the likely reason:

> Matthew obviously did not list every individual in the genealogy between Abraham and David (vv. 2-6), between David and the Exile (vv. 6-11), and between the Exile and Jesus (vv. 12-16). Instead, he listed only *fourteen* generations in each of these time periods (v. 17). Jewish reckoning did not require every name in order to satisfy a

genealogy. But why did Matthew select *fourteen* names in each period? "David" in Hebrew numerology added up to *fourteen*.[4]

David is a lovely type of the Greater David who would eventually come to fulfill all of the Abrahamic covenant and be David's rightful heir to his throne forever. Hebrew numbers are composed of a series of letters and David's name (*dvd* in Hebrew) equates to the number *fourteen* (*dalet* = 4, *vav* = 6, and *dalet* = 4 for a total of *fourteen*). *Fourteen* is symbolic of salvation and deliverance in Scripture. As discussed previously, the number *three* represents *resurrection* and *completeness*. By repeating the number *fourteen* thrice, the Holy Spirit is telling us the Jesus Christ is the ultimate Deliverer of humanity – only in Him is there complete salvation of the human spirit, soul, and body (1 Cor. 6:20; 1 Thess. 5:23). The complete salvation requires resurrection and will therefore be complete at the believer's glorification when Christ comes back for His Church (1 Cor. 15:51-52; 1 Thess. 4:13-18).

Through Jesus Christ, we can rejoice that our souls are saved from the *penalty of sin*, and through the Holy Spirit we now have *power over sin*. Furthermore, we are to anticipate a future day when we will be saved from the *presence of sin*. At that moment a believer's body will be transformed into holy humanity – like Christ's body (Phil. 3:20-21). In Christ, a believer has been saved (John 5:24; Eph. 2:8), is being saved (Phil. 2:12; Rom. 8:24), and will be saved (Rom. 13:11; 1 Thess. 5:9). Through trusting Jesus Christ alone for salvation, we experience a trifold-saving, which will completely deliver us from sin and this corrupt world.

Ivan Panin, further describes the unique construction of Matthew's record of Christ's genealogy by highlighting the prevalent occurrence of the number *seven* throughout the Greek text. For example, in the first section (vv. 1-11) there are: 49 words (7x7), 28 (7x4) of these words begin with a vowel and 21 (7x3) with a consonant. These 49 words contain 266 (7x38) letters. Of these 266 letters, 140 (7x20) are vowels and 126 (7x18) are consonants. Of the 49 words in this text, 35 words (7x5) occur more than once and 14 (7x2) occur only once. Concerning the parts of speech, 42 (7x6) are nouns and 7 are not nouns and 35 (7x5) of the nouns are proper names. In fact, God's number of perfection is used in a prominent way throughout the remainder of Matthew 1, which addresses the genealogy and birth of Christ.[5]

Bible Numbers and Symbols

Sometime after Paul's conversion on the road to Damascus, he visited the church in Jerusalem, and shared his story with some of the apostles (Acts 9:26-30; Gal. 1:18-20). He made a second trip to Jerusalem for the purpose of famine relief (Acts 11:27-30). Then, *fourteen* years after his initial visit, he returned to Jerusalem again (Gal. 2:1-10) to discuss the negative influence of Jewish legalizers on Gentile believers. While this trip may be the same as the famine relief visit, the subject matter Paul was discussing perfectly agrees with the purpose of the Jerusalem Council held in 49 A.D. (Acts 15:1-30). If this assumption is correct, Paul's conversion would have occurred one to two years after Christ's crucifixion; this timing fits well with the historical account in the book of Acts, as Paul would have just completed His first missionary journey with Barnabas. The *fourteenth* time Paul's name is mentioned in Scripture (i.e., in the book of Acts) is while he is attending the Jerusalem Council (Acts 15:2), which apparently was *fourteen* years after his previous visit to Jerusalem. Just before the fifteenth mention of Paul's name (Acts 15:12), the clear conclusion of the debate is stated: salvation is solely through grace and in Christ alone:

> *Now therefore, why do you test God by putting a yoke on the neck of the disciples which neither our fathers nor we were able to bear? But we believe that through the grace of the Lord Jesus Christ we shall be saved in the same manner as they"* (Acts 15:10-11).

The number *fourteen* is connected with God's complete *deliverance* and *salvation* offered through Christ in Scripture.

Fifteen – Rest

The number *fifteen* (including *fifteenth*) is only found 35 times as a standalone number in Scripture. Just as the number *fifteen* follows *fourteen*, so does rest and peace naturally ensue after one has received God's salvation in Christ. The Jews were to keep seven Feasts of Jehovah (Lev. 23). The second feast to be kept was The Feast of Unleavened Bread, which was on the *fifteenth* day of the first month and followed on the next day after the Passover. The Passover celebrated Israel's deliverance from Egypt through the applied blood of the Passover lamb (Ex. 12). The *fifteenth* day was to be a day of holy convocation – *a complete rest* from all laboring.

The seventh feast in the Jewish calendar was The Feast of Tabernacles held on the *fifteenth* day of the seventh month; it also was a day of holy convocation – *a day of rest*. This feast fell on the heels of the Day of Atonement, which is when the High Priest offered the blood of a bullock and a goat to atone for the sins of Israel, not already dealt with by other atonement rituals. No blood atonement for sin meant that fellowship with God could not be enjoyed, meaning that the blessings and rest associated with His presence would be lost.

A third example of the symbolic meaning of *fifteen* is found in the book of Esther, after the Jews had experienced God's great deliverance from Haman's evil plot to exterminate them. Esther's uncle Mordecai had been highly exalted in the Persian court because of his faithfulness to the king and his honorable character. He sent a decree to all the Jews throughout the Persian Empire to have an annual feast, called Purim, to recall God's salvation and rest (Est. 9:20-22). This feast was to be held in the month of Adar on the *fourteenth* and *fifteenth* days, which represent the ideas of deliverance and rest, respectively.

Sixteen – Love

Yahweh is translated as "Jehovah" in some English versions of the Bible, but normally it is rendered as "the Lord" or "O Lord." *Yahweh* is rendered from the Hebrew tetragrammaton YHWH and represents God's personal name as revealed to Israel. Yahweh is found nearly 7,000 times in the Old Testament and most likely relates to the verb "to be": Yahweh is the eternal, immutable, and self-existing Creator of all things. In Exodus 3:14, the Lord declares to Moses, *"I AM THAT I AM."* Besides being self-existing, John tells us that God is characterized by love, *"for God is love"* (1 Jn. 4:8).

The number *sixteen* (including *sixteenth*) is found only 22 times as a standalone number in the Bible. However, there are *sixteen* times in the Old Testament that Jehovah's name is combined with specific thoughts as to who He is and what He does. These are called Jehovah Titles and are expressions of majestic love to His covenant people and to us too:

1. Jehovah Elohim – The eternal One (Gen. 2:4-5)
2. Jehovah Adonai – The Lord our sovereign; Master (Gen. 15:2, 8)
3. Jehovah Jireh – The Lord will see or provide (Gen. 22:8-14)
4. Jehovah Nissi – The Lord our banner (Ex. 17:15)

Bible Numbers and Symbols

5. Jehovah Rapha – The Lord our healer (Ex. 15:26)
6. Jehovah Shalom – The Lord our peace (Judg. 6:24)
7. Jehovah Tsidkenu – The Lord our righteousness (Jer. 23:6, 33:16)
8. Jehovah Mekaddishkem – The Lord our sanctifier (Ex. 31:13)
9. Jehovah Sabaoth – The Lord of hosts (1 Sam. 1:3)
10. Jehovah Shammah – The Lord is present (Ezek. 48:35)
11. Jehovah Elyon – The Lord most high (Ps. 7:17, 47:2, 97:9)
12. Jehovah Rohi – The Lord my shepherd (Ps. 23:1)
13. Jehovah Hoseenu – The Lord our maker (Ps. 95:6)
14. Jehovah Eloheka – The Lord your God (Ex. 20:2, 5, 7)
15. Jehovah Elohay – The Lord my God (Zech. 14:5)
16. Jehovah Eloheenu – The Lord our God (Ps. 99:5, 8, 9)

In 1 Corinthians 13, Paul teaches us that biblical love should govern the use of our spiritual gifts in serving others. Biblical love is selfless and self-sacrificing. The Corinthian believers were being selfish and self-focused in the use of their spiritual abilities. If what we do for the Lord is not motivated by genuine love, it means nothing (1 Cor. 13:1-3). The apostle describes *sixteen* characteristics of what selfless love is and what it is not:

What love is:	**What love is not:**
Suffers long – it is patient	Does not envy – rejoices when others are honored
Kind – tender and compassionate	Does not boast of self – quiet with own accomplishments
Centers in the truth – rejoices in it	Not proud – all abilities come from God
Bears all things – commitment based	Keeps no list of wrongs
Believes the positive possibility first	Does not seek self-interest above others
Hopes – rejoices in God's promises	Not easily provoked to anger
Endures – longsuffering of offenses	Does not rejoice in sin or failures of others
God's love is inexhaustible/eternal	Does not think evil – thinks positively or gives the benefit of the doubt

Because the source of true love is God, all that His love motivates will reflect the fruit of the Holy Spirit. Biblical love is sacrificial by nature: *"For God so loved the world that He gave His only begotten Son"* (John 3:16). The only way that we can love others as God loves is to experience His selfless, sacrificial love: *"We love because He first loved us"* (1 Jn. 4:19).

Sixteen is the product of *two* and *eight*. *Two* may represent the testimony of *division* (distinction) or the testimony of *union*, while the number *eight* speaks of *new beginnings* (such as being born again). The choice is ours. Will we, as believers in Christ, cause division in the Body that contains all those who have been born again, or will we enhance Body-life in Christ by sharing His love?

Seventeen – Victory

While the number *seventeen* (including *seventeenth*) is only found 12 times in Scripture as a standalone number, its mathematical uniqueness provides some insight as to its spiritual meaning. The *sixth* prime number (i.e., a number not divisible by any other whole number but itself and one) is *thirteen*. *Six* is the number of man and *thirteen* the number of rebellion; hence, human insurrection is especially associated with the number *thirteen*.

Seventeen is the *seventh* prime number and therefore we would also expect it to reflect some quality of divine *completeness* and *perfection* in its meaning. Additionally, the number *seventeen* is also the sum of two perfect numbers *ten* and *seven*. *Seven* is God's number of *perfection* and *completeness* and *ten* is His number of *divine testimony* (especially, that which puts man under obligation). Indeed, the spiritual meaning of *seventeen* found in Scripture is the idea of victory, especially the complete victory in Christ that all believers enjoy.

We find an application of the meaning of *seventeen*, even before the number appears on the holy page, in Genesis 7:11. In Genesis 5, we have the genealogy of Seth recorded. We read of a godly man named Enoch who "walked with God" for 300 years (Gen. 5:22). Enoch had a son named Methuselah, who lived longer than any other man on record – 969 years (Gen. 5:27). When Methuselah was 187 years old, he had a son named Lamech (Gen. 5:25). When Lamech was 182 years old, he had a son named Noah, who also walked with God (Gen. 5:28, 6:6). Lamech lived another 595 years after Noah was born (Gen. 5:30).

In a mysterious way, the birth of Methuselah was a prophecy in itself – Methuselah's name means "when it comes." God was telling Enoch that as long as his son lived, the world would live, but when his son died, the world would die. So, when did Methuselah die? Methuselah was 187 years old when his son Lamech was born, and Lamech was 182 years old when Noah was born. Noah was 600 years old when the flood came (7:6). Consequently, Methuselah was 969 (187 + 182 + 600) years old when the flood came, and Scripture records that he lived 969 years – he died the year the flood occurred. Literally, the prophecy of his name was fulfilled "when it came." After Noah's birth, Lamech lived another 595 years, which means he died five years before the flood.

Notice now how God marked Noah for victory – to escape the flood by God's means of deliverance. The 969-year lifespan of Methuselah (which was to identify when the flood would occur) is divisible by seventeen as is Noah's age when his father Lamech died (595). Lamech was not the one chosen to escape the flood, but his son Noah was. Not only does Methuselah's age demonstrate God's longsuffering nature, but also there is no other individual in the Bible whose lifespan is divisible by seventeen.

Building the ark, as God commanded, took Noah and his family many years and then they had to care for all the creatures in the ark for over another year. Through God's ark, Noah and his family achieved a great victory – a new life in a new world. In fact, the ark floated safely off the Earth on the *seventeenth* day of the *second* month and rested on the mountains of Ararat on the *seventeenth* day of the *seventh* month (Gen. 7:11, 8:4). The sea journey that Noah's family undertook began with victorious division (the meaning of *two* and *seventeen*) from the Earth and ended with complete victory (the meaning of *seven* and *seventeen*).

There were *eight* souls saved by the ark and *eight* is the number of *new beginnings*. Likewise, we are more than conquerors in Christ, when we exercise obedience and faith in God's Word just as Noah did (Rom. 8:37). In Christ we have new life – victorious resurrection power through and through. In Christ, we enjoy a new beginning and eternal victory (2 Cor. 5:8)!

Another lovely picture of *victory* conveyed through the number *seventeen* is found in the Exodus 14 narrative. The Israelites were liberated from Egypt and slavery on the fourteenth day of the first month by applying the blood of the Passover lamb.

Once freed, the Israelites traveled southeast from Rameses and encamped at Succoth, then at Etham, and then at Pi Hahiroth just west of the Red Sea. This was apparently the third day after Passover, the *seventeenth* day of the month. They soon were entrapped at this position by the Egyptian army. However, that evening the Lord parted the sea to provide a way of escape for His people. He also used the sea to wipe out Israel's pursuing enemy, which prompted them to sing to the Lord, *"For He has triumphed gloriously! The horse and its rider He has thrown into the sea!"* (Ex. 15:1). They had been redeemed and liberated while in Egypt, but now the enemy who sought to wipe them out would bother them no more – full victory had been achieved.

This historical picture wonderfully typifies the death and resurrection of the Lord Jesus, God's Passover Lamb for humanity (1 Cor. 5:7). The Lord was put to death at Passover, the *fourteenth* day of the first month, and then was raised from the grave in ultimate victory three days later! As Paul notes, all believers in Christ share in His victory:

> *So when this corruptible has put on incorruption, and this mortal has put on immortality, then shall be brought to pass the saying that is written: "Death is swallowed up in victory." "O Death, where is your sting? O Hades, where is your victory?" The sting of death is sin, and the strength of sin is the law. But thanks be to God, who gives us the victory through our Lord Jesus Christ* (1 Cor. 15:54-57).

Another typological application of the number *seventeen* is found in the life of Joseph in the book of Genesis. Joseph had already revealed the meaning of his dreams to his brothers. But they rejected his claims of leadership and envied him because of the special relationship he enjoyed with their father Jacob. When Joseph was *seventeen*, Jacob sent him to find his older brothers who were remotely attending to his flocks. His brothers initially restrained Joseph in a pit and then sold him to some Ishmaelites for twenty shekels of silver. He was subsequently taken to Egypt and sold as a slave (Gen. 37). Joseph is an astounding type of Christ and these events foreshadow Christ's first advent to the Earth. Being about His Father's business, He was rejected by Israel, crucified, place in a grave (a pit), but then was raised up and removed from the presence of His brethren.

After thirteen years of hardship, Joseph was appointed by Pharaoh to be the second ruler in Egypt in order to preserve the land through the terrible seven-year famine that was coming. This was the meaning of Pharaoh's dreams that Joseph foretold by God's help. This pictures the future Tribulation Period that will threaten Israel's existence under the rule of the Antichrist. But Christ will preserve and refine Israel during this time and then they will enjoy the blessings of the Kingdom Age.

Jacob, also called "Israel," came to Egypt during the second year of the famine; he was 130 years old at that time and he lived to be 147 years of age (Gen. 47:28). Israel was in the land under Joseph's care for *seventeen* years. This second reference to *seventeen* in the life of Joseph foretells Christ's second advent. Both advents are marked by victory. In His first coming, Christ brought victory over sin and death and in His second He will deliver those who are His from all oppression and then they will be greatly blessed in Christ's kingdom.

Lastly, Psalm 83 lists *seventeen* enemies of Israel that God will overcome on behalf of His people (Ps. 83:6-11). The psalm acknowledges God's past victories over the Midianites, Sisera, Jabin, Oreb, Zeeb, Zebah and Zalmunna and then anticipates how the Lord will defeat Israel's future enemies in the same way: The Edomites, Ishmaelites, Moabites, Hagrites, Gebalites, Ammonites, Amalekites, Philistines, and those from Tyre and Assyria are mentioned. God's people in any era have complete victory in the Lord!

Eighteen – Bondage

The number *eighteen* (including *eighteenth*) is found only 24 times as a standalone number in the Bible. It is mainly through observing the *eighteenth* instance of something in a particular book of Scripture or that there are only *eighteen* occurrences of some aspect in Scripture that we may infer its meaning.

Through a vision, the Lord foretold to Abram the harsh events and then the deliverance that his descendants would experience:

> *Then He said to Abram: "Know certainly that your descendants will be strangers in a land that is not theirs, and will serve them, and they will afflict them four hundred years. And also the nation whom they serve I will judge; afterward they shall come out with great possessions* (Gen. 15:13-14).

The Holy Spirit then inspired different writers to use some form of the Hebrew word *abad*, translated "bondage," *eighteen* times in the Old Testament to confirm that what God said would happen to Israel (as pertaining to Egyptian oppression) – did happen: Exodus 1:14, 2:23 (twice), 6:5, 6:6, 6:9, 13:3, 13:14, 20:2; Deuteronomy 5:6, 6:12, 7:8, 8:14, 13:5, 13:10, 26:6; Joshua 24:17; and Judges 6:8. In Judges 6:8, the *eighteenth* reference to Israel's bondage in Egypt we find Israel in servitude again, but to a different people group – they served the Midianites for seven years. Here the number *seven* seems to mark the completeness of God's discussion of Israel's Egyptian bondage. The next time Scripture speaks of Israel being in bondage is in the book of Ezra, which relates to their Babylonian captivity.

During the era of the Judges, Israel was often chastened by the Lord for their idolatry. The Jews would be oppressed by foreign people for a period of time before God raised up a judge to deliver them from their bondage. For example, the Lord used the Moabites for *eighteen* years and then the Philistines for *eighteen* years to punish His covenant people in this way (Judg. 3:14, 10:7-8).

In the *eighteenth* year of King Josiah's reign, the book of the Law was found in the temple and then read to the king by the scribe Shaphan (2 Kg. 22:3). Josiah asked for the priests to seek counsel from the Lord how to best resolve the offense of Israel's negligence, for he realized that by not keeping the Law, they had aroused God's great wrath against them (2 Kgs. 22:13). That wrath had repeatedly been expressed through the invasion, oppression, and enslavement of Israel by foreign nations.

Luke records the Lord Jesus healing a woman who had been bound by an infirmity for *eighteen* years and also His rebuke to those disapproving of the miracle because it occurred on the Sabbath:

> *Now He was teaching in one of the synagogues on the Sabbath. And behold, there was a woman **who had a spirit of infirmity eighteen years**, and was bent over and could in no way raise herself up. But when Jesus saw her, He called her to Him and said to her, "Woman, you are loosed from your infirmity." And He laid His hands on her, and immediately she was made straight, and glorified God. But the ruler of the synagogue answered with indignation, because Jesus had healed on the Sabbath; and he said to the crowd, "There are six days on which men ought to work; therefore come and be healed on them, and not on the Sabbath day." The Lord then answered him and said, "Hypocrite! Does not each one of you on the Sabbath loose his ox or donkey from the stall, and lead it away to water it? So ought not this woman, being a daughter of Abraham, **whom Satan has bound** – think of it – **for eighteen years, be loosed from this bond** on the Sabbath?"* (Luke 13:10-16).

Likewise, only through Christ can those who are enslaved by sin and caught in Satan's death-grip be liberated to praise God and serve Him willingly.

Nineteen – Faith

We only find *nineteen* (including the *nineteenth*) 6 times in Scripture as a standalone number, all of which are in the Old Testament. Of these references, only one event is mentioned twice – the destruction of Jerusalem and the temple by Nebuchadnezzar's Babylonian army in 586 B.C. Both 2 Kings 25:8 and Jeremiah 52:12 recorded that this catastrophic event, which had been previously foretold by the prophet Jeremiah, occurred in the *nineteenth* year of Nebuchadnezzar's reign.

Sinful behavior is a matter that God cannot ignore in His people. It must be judged. There was a dark and ominous cloud approaching Israel, but the Jews largely ignored Jeremiah's message of impending doom (Jer. 13:16-17). Jeremiah appealed to the king (likely Jehoiachin) to humble himself by laying aside his regal splendor and accepting God's judgment (Jer. 13:17-18). If he resisted the Babylonian army, it would not go well for him or his people. If he surrendered to the invasion force, many lives would be saved (Jer. 13:18-21). But Jeremiah's offer of life, which required Judah's chastening in Babylon, was refused by the king.

This same ultimatum was later affirmed to King Zedekiah (Jer. 21:9). Jeremiah pleaded with his countrymen not to resist the will of God, but to willingly surrender to the Babylonians and live. If they did not surrender, God promised to fight against them and they would die. Zedekiah did not heed this warning, which brought devasting consequences to Israel. After Jerusalem finally succumbed to its long siege, so many Jews were slaughtered by the Babylonians that proper burial of their dead corpses was not possible; as Jeremiah had foretold, the wild animals devoured their remains.

The bright spot in all of this is that some Jews, did heed Jeremiah's message and in faith defected to Babylon and lived. *"The defectors who had deserted to the king of Babylon"* were *"carried away captive"* to Babylon (Jer. 52:15). As Jeremiah and Isaiah prophesied, many of their descendants, after seventy years' captivity in Babylon, would be liberated and return to Jerusalem to rebuild the temple – a new testimony of Jehovah's greatness (Jer. 25:12; Isa. 44:28). These events demonstrate that though exercising faith in God's Word may result in sobering consequences, the outcome of doing so provides an honorable testimony of God's goodness to others. Exercising faith in God's Word is always the best way to enjoy life, that is, to live with and for God.

This is the central message of the Great Faith Hall of Fame chapter – Hebrews 11. Its theme is introduced in Hebrews 10:38: *"The just shall live by faith."* Then we read the expression "by faith" *nineteen* times in Hebrews 11 to describe the various individuals who chose to *live by faith* and were consequently powerfully used by God. Like the prophet Habakkuk, who the writer of Hebrews quotes, we may not understand what God is doing, but whatever it is, we just need to trust Him, for He knows how to work all things for a greater good (Rom. 8:28).

Under the Law, the Jews were to demonstrate their faith in Jehovah by keeping His annual feasts (Lev. 23). These seven feasts consisted of *nineteen* holy days: Passover (1), Unleavened Bread (7), Pentecost (1), Trumpets (1), Day of Atonement (1), Feast of Tabernacles (7) and Last Great Day (1).

Paul tells us, *"For by grace you have been saved through faith"* (Eph. 2:8). The number of *grace* is *five*, and the number of *salvation* is *fourteen*, and their sum is *nineteen*, *faith*.

Twenty – Redemption

Unlike the number *nineteen*, which is rarely found in Scripture, we observe the number *twenty* (or *twentieth*) as a standalone number 157 times. The number *twenty* is largely associated with the idea of *redemption* in Scripture. Silver is a metal that also symbolizes redemption in the Bible, so these two metaphors are often connected together.

Although redemption is an obvious prerequisite to being able to worship God acceptably, the discussion of the Jewish men *twenty* years of age and older paying atonement money poses a difficulty to our minds (Ex. 30:11-16). If the newly liberated Jewish nation had been redeemed by the blood of the Passover lamb in Egypt, why did Jehovah command Moses to tell the people in the wilderness that *"every man shall give a ransom for himself to the Lord"* (Ex. 30:12). How can a man give a ransom for himself if true redemption is only through the precious blood of Christ (1 Pet. 1:18-19)?

The answer to this apparent contradiction is found in the specific language of the command itself: *"**When** you take the census of the

Bible Numbers and Symbols

children of Israel for their number, ***then*** *every man shall give a ransom for himself to the Lord,* ***when*** *you number them, that there may be no plague among them when you number them"* (v. 12). The ransom money (a half shekel of silver) was to be paid by every adult man (*twenty* years of age or older) when the census of the people was accomplished. A census would be required before the Israelites could worship God; and then years later, a second census would be performed just before the Israelites entered the Promised Land.

Moses, picturing Christ, was God's mediator for the people; when he numbered the children of Israel, he was simply appropriating to God the sum of those who had already been redeemed. By counting all of the men, God demonstrated His ownership over the entire nation. The firstborns, however, had been redeemed in Egypt by God's Passover and were thus representative of the entire nation. The act of adult men paying the ransom money showed everyone that, indeed, God had *appropriated* the entire nation to Himself, not just the firstborns. The redeemed were to stand up and be counted; the atonement money was their acknowledgment to the Lord that they had been redeemed and that He owned them. Thus, the atonement money represented what God had already accomplished, rather than actually effecting atonement itself.

When it comes to redemption, every human is worth the same to God: *"The rich shall not give more and the poor shall not give less than half a shekel, when you give an offering to the Lord, to make atonement for yourselves"* (Ex. 30:15). All were to pay alike. Why were pieces of silver used for ransom money? As previously mentioned, silver symbolizes redemption in Scripture; in fact, the Lord Jesus was betrayed for thirty pieces of silver, which later the Pharisees referred to as "blood money." The pieces of silver were connected with the means of our ransom – Christ's own redeeming blood.

The tabernacle consisted of a framework of forty-eight boards overlaid with gold. The bottom of each board had two tenons which stood in a silver base-plate of ninety-six sockets. The boards were then braced together by gold-covered rods of wood (five for each wall). Without the silver sockets, the tabernacle would have no footing on which to erect walls. The silver to form these sockets came from the people when they were numbered and paid the ransom money. The entire activity of counting and paying the silver was God's official acknowledgment that all of the Israelites were a ransomed people. Jehovah wanted all of His people to understand that only through redemption could they offer acceptable worship to Him at the tabernacle – the same is still true today in the heavenly sense.

We read the name of Ruth's kinsman-redeemer, Boaz, *twenty* times in the book of Ruth. He was the only one who was both willing and able to redeem Ruth with the land associated with Naomi's dead husband. Christ is the only one willing and able to redeem our souls to God. Barley, which is also a symbol of redemption in Scripture (see Hos. 3:2), is mentioned more times in the short book of Ruth than any other book of the Bible. Ruth, a Moabite, was diligently gleaning barley for her and her mother-in-law when she received unmerited favor from Boaz (Ruth 2:10).

Twenty-One – Wickedness and Sinfulness

The number *twenty-one* (or *twenty-first*) is only found 8 times in the Bible as a standalone number. Its meaning is probably best understood in the product of itself and another number with which it seems to be linked, the number *thirteen*. This will be explained momentarily. As already observed, the number *thirteen* relates to *rebellion* and *depravity*. The number *twenty-one* seems to represent the outcome of such a rebellious disposition towards God – the *exceeding sinfulness* of sin.

Paul acknowledges the sobering effect that God's Law had on him; it brought out the worst of his fallen nature. Instead of causing him to hate what God said not to do, he found that he just wanted to do it more. The problem was not with God's holy standard, but his depraved nature:

> *Has then what is good* [speaking of the Law] *become death to me? Certainly not! But sin, that it might appear sin, was producing death in me through what is good, so that sin through the commandment might become exceedingly sinful. For we know that the law is spiritual, but I am carnal, sold under sin* (Rom. 7:13-14).

The product of *thirteen* and *twenty-one* is *two hundred seventy-three*; this number is found in Numbers 3. There was a census to be performed so that God could dedicate the Levites to Himself for service in the tabernacle instead of the firstborn males redeemed by the blood of the Passover Lamb (Num. 3:40-51).

The census showed that the number of the firstborn in Israel (born after the Exodus) exceeded the number of the Levite males by 273. This meant there were not enough Levites to redeem all the firstborn males.

Bible Numbers and Symbols

We might understand the transaction this way: Why would God trade more of anything for less of the same thing? That would not be an equitable exchange. However, the Lord claimed these 273 equally with the 22,000 for whom a Levite was found as a substitute, and thus five shekels of silver had to be paid for each of the 273 needing to be redeemed. The principle of redemption before us is not positional, but provisional for service, for all Israel had been positionally redeemed by blood in Egypt. The firstborns who had survived the tenth plague were a constant reminder of the positional redemption that the nation had already received.

The redemption money was collected by Aaron the high priest to illustrate God's acceptance and claim on the redeemed Levites to serve and worship Him on behalf of the nation. Considering the deplorable behavior of Levi in Genesis 34, this is a wonderful testimony of what can be accomplished by God's grace through redemption. By nature, Levi had been an instrument of cruelty, but by grace he was a vessel serving in God's sanctuary!

Again, the idea of redemption in Numbers 3 pertains to the opportunity to serve God; it is not speaking of the initial act of positional recovery. What God redeems, He further sanctifies for His glory. Not only were the Levites redeemed, but they now had the opportunity to come near God in service and to worship. Thank the Lord that He is willing and able to redeem what is inherently depraved in nature and capable of exceeding sinfulness for His honor and glory.

Interestingly, three of the four times that the number *twenty-one* is found in Scripture, it is associated with the last king to sit on Judah's throne, Zedekiah. He was a wicked king who defied God, His Word, and wronged His prophets. He was *twenty-one* years old when he became king (2 Kgs. 24:18; 2 Chron. 36:11; Jer. 52:1). He represents the apex of Israel's rebellion against God – the *exceeding sinfulness of sin*. When the Babylonians conquered Jerusalem, all of Zedekiah's sons were executed before him, and then the Babylonians put his eyes out and hauled him away to Babylon where he died. No king has ever sat on Israel's throne since then and none will until the "time of the Gentiles" concludes at the second advent of the Lord Jesus Christ (Luke 21:24).

The fourth time that the number *twenty-one* is found in Scripture relates to a wicked angel hindering a less-powerful, holy angel from delivering a message to Daniel for *twenty-one* days (Dan. 10:13).

Michael, the archangel, intervened to enable the hindered angel to deliver his message to Daniel.

The number *twenty-one* represents wickedness, and Paul identifies *twenty-one* specific sins in 2 Timothy 3:2-4 which characterize humanity in the latter days of the Church Age. It has become quite evident that this spirit of lawlessness is already ramping up today!

Twenty-Two – Light

The number *twenty-two* is more often compounded with other numbers in Scripture than occurring by itself. We find *twenty-two* (including *twenty-second*) standing alone a mere 11 times in the Bible. Its metaphoric meaning of *light* is derived mainly from the divine instructions given Moses concerning the construction of the Golden Lampstand in the Holy Place of the tabernacle (Ex. 25:31-40).

The Lampstand was to be formed from one solid piece of pure gold that weighed one talent (75 to 100 pounds). It was not to be forged, but beaten into perfection. The Lampstand consisted of a central stem with three branches springing out from each side to form a total of seven branches. Each side branch was to have three almond flower-shaped bowls (cups), while the central stem was to have four similar bowls, which meant that there was a total of twenty-two bowls in the structure of the Lampstand. The seven burning lamps, one on top of each side branch and the central stem, was the only source of light in the tabernacle.

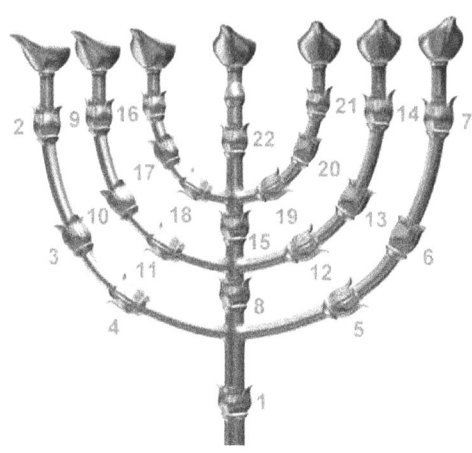

Metaphorically, light in Scripture symbolizes the truth and holiness of God, and, as these are non-varying, eternal qualities, the Lampstand was always lit when the tabernacle was operational. The light of the Lampstand was produced by seven ever-burning wicks; each wick drew a constant supply of fine olive oil from its reservoir. The priests entered into the Holy Place twice a day for the morning and evening offerings. Besides placing hot coals and specially prepared incense upon the Golden Altar, the priests also trimmed the seven wicks of the Lampstand and, as needed, filled its reservoirs with oil (Ex. 27:20-21; Lev. 24:4).

As already observed, the number *seven* is God's number signifying *spiritual perfection* and *holiness*. Through the number *seven*, the light of the Lampstand, which represents Christ's testimony of truth is shown to be divine in origin. Likewise, the resource enabling the seven flames to illuminate the tabernacle (the oil) is also shown to be divine in nature. As in Zechariah's vision of the two olive trees that supplied oil to a lampstand, the Holy Spirit is also in Exodus 27 depicted in the pure oil. Speaking of the oil, the Lord told Zechariah: *"Not by might nor by power, but by My Spirit"* (Zech. 4:6). God was confirming that it would be His Spirit working in Joshua and Zerubbabel (the two trees) to accomplish His will and provide a testimony of Himself in Jerusalem. The Lampstand in the tabernacle, then, speaks of God's perfect revelation of truth in Christ through the power of the Holy Spirit.

The Golden Lampstand was a unique article; there was nothing else like it, and so is its connection with the number *twenty-two*. There is nothing else in Scripture in which the number *twenty-two* is closely associated. Putting all of these types together, we understand that the resurrection life of Christ, the truth of Christ, and the Holy Spirit all reside in the believer today. Consequently, as the believer remains in fellowship with Christ and chooses to live for Him, a world filled with satanic darkness becomes illuminated with divine truth. The life of Christ must be lived out and this is only possible by yielding to divine truth. Not living according to divine truth grieves the Holy Spirit and thus diminishes His supernatural enablement in our lives. Each believer is called to be a living lampstand for Christ.

Scripture affixes Lampstand responsibility on both individual believers (Matt. 5:14) and local churches (Rev. 1:20). Light testifies of divine truth and of divine power in action. Only as believers are enabled by the Holy Spirit can they *shine out* a testimony of Christ's life within. Paul refers to believers as "children of light" (1 Thess. 5:5). When someone experiences the number *fourteen*, *salvation* in Christ, the number *eight* – *a new beginning* in Christ through the power of the Holy Spirit – also occurs. The sum of *eight* and *fourteen* must be *twenty-two* – God illuminates the believer's life with divine *light*!

Twenty-Three – Death

The number *twenty-three* (including *twenty-third*) is only found 13 times in the Bible as a standalone number. *Twenty-three* is the sum of *ten*, representing the testimony of God's Law, and *thirteen*, the number of rebellion. Paul clearly connects these two ideas together: *"The sting of death is sin, and the strength of sin is the law"* (1 Cor. 15:56).

The message of the Law is that God will judge all that offends His holy character and that everyone falls short of His perfect standard (Rom. 3:19-20, 23). Thankfully, Scripture presents a solution to sin and death: *"For the wages of sin is death, but the gift of God is eternal life in Christ Jesus our Lord"* (Rom. 6:23). In Adam, we are all born with a depraved nature, as "children of wrath" (Eph. 2:3), and thus stand condemned before God (John 3:18). The Law examines our behavior to confirm this is true and then points us to God's solution for sin and death – Christ (Gal. 3:24). Only in Christ can we be saved from eternal death!

Although God revealed Himself to natural man through creation (Rom. 1:20), many choose to ignore this revelation and not *"retain God in their knowledge"* (Rom. 1:28). Because they chose to worship God's creation (including themselves) and not the Creator, *"God gave them over to a debased mind, to do those things which are not fitting"* (Rom. 1:28). Sin begets more sin; hence, Paul lists twenty-two sins following those committing the first sin of rejecting God's revealed righteousness (Rom. 1:29-31). The apostle then concludes by stating: *"that those who practice such things are deserving of death"* (Rom. 1:32). Sin results in death – separation from God! This thought is expressed concisely in Judges 10:2; *"He* [Abimelech] *judged Israel twenty-three years; and he died."* The judicial consequence of sin is death.

A second equation resulting in *twenty-three* that involves one of the four perfect numbers is the summation of *three*, the number of *divine perfection and resurrection*, and the number *twenty*, the number of *redemption*. When Christ returns to the air for His Church, all that were dead will experience resurrection and those believers still alive on Earth will experience glorification. The latter saints will likely pass through death instantaneously to receive an eternal, Christ-like, incorruptible body (1 Cor. 15:51-52; Phil. 3:21; 1 Thess. 4:13-18; Heb. 9:27). Paul refers to this as the salvation of the body (Rom. 13:11), for it is saved out of the presence of sin forever. Believers are fully redeemed by the blood of Christ, spirit, soul, and body (1 Cor. 6:20; 1 Thess. 5:23). At the rapture of the Church, believers will receive glorified bodies that will make them fit for heaven!

A third equation resulting in *twenty-three* that again involves one of the four perfect numbers is the summation of *eleven*, the number of *judgment*, and the number *twelve*, the number of *divine administration and authority*. We will now examine Romans 1:32 more fully: *"Who, knowing the righteous judgment of God* [i.e., knowing that God is Judge]*, that those who practice such things are deserving of death, not only do the same but also approve of those who practice them."* God's solution to man's sin is displayed in Christ, and hence it is Christ who will judge those deserving death, those who rejected Him (John 5:22; Phil. 2:10).

The last equation resulting in *twenty-three*, which employs a perfect number, is the summation of *seven*, God's number of *spiritual completeness and perfection* and the number *sixteen*, the number of *love*. As John explains, God the Father demonstrated His great love for us by giving His Son to reverse the death and destruction caused by human sin:

> *For God so loved the world that He gave His only begotten Son, that whoever believes in Him should not perish but have everlasting life. For God did not send His Son into the world to condemn the world, but that the world through Him might be saved. He who believes in Him is not condemned; but he who does not believe is condemned already, because he has not believed in the name of the only begotten Son of God* (John 3:16-18).

In the number *twenty-three*, we find the devastating effects of human sin and its result – *death*. God's righteous Law identifies sin, and God being a righteous Judge must judge sin. However, God's immense love in Christ expresses the only remedy for sin and death, redemption through Christ. A holy God must judge sin, but a loving God found a righteous way of doing so that wonderfully demonstrates that He is a God of love.

The number *twenty-three* seemingly represents *death*. It is observed that the *twenty-third* time Abraham's name appears in Genesis, he is observing the smoke rising from the Jordanian cities that God judged with fire (Gen. 19:27-28). The *twenty-third* time Jacob's name appears in Genesis is when his mother Rebekah informs him of his brother Esau's vow to put him to death (Gen. 27:42). Directly after the *twenty-third* time that Peter's name is found in the book of Acts, we read of the death of Dorcas, also called Tabitha (Acts 9:34-37).

Mordecai, under the authority of King Ahasuerus, wrote a decree on the *twenty-third* day of the third month that permitted the Jews to protect themselves against Haman's edict that sought their eradication throughout the Persian Empire (Est. 8:9-11).

Twenty-Four – The Priesthood

The number *twenty-four* (including *twenty-fourth*) is found as a standalone number 20 times in the Bible. The number *twenty-four* is clearly associated with God's appointed *priesthood* in Scripture. Because of a divinely approved position, a priest may represent others before God and offer acceptable worship to God.

Because of the large number of Levites in his day, David divided God's ministers into *twenty-four* orders, each division waiting for their opportunity to serve before the Lord in the tabernacle, and then the temple. Aaron was the first High Priest, and only his descendants could officiate the Levitical offerings and sacrifices. Accordingly, each of Aaron's *twenty-four* descendants (through his sons Eleazar and Ithamar) became the heads of each priestly order (1 Chron. 24:1-19). The Levites, who were to assist the priests and attend to the logistics of temple operations, were also divided into *twenty-four* distinct groups (1 Chron. 24:20-31). The *twenty-four* priestly orders also included the temple singers (1 Chron. 6:32). Each of these *twenty-four* divisions was then assigned a schedule to serve before the Lord on a rotating basis (1 Chron. 24:4, 19). This meant that each household would serve at the temple about two weeks a year.

The number *twenty-four*, as implicated in 1 Chronicles 24, is associated with priestly service. In John's vision of heaven, *twenty-four* elders are sitting on thrones in heaven about God's throne; these represent redeemed souls which God has made to be kings and priests in His presence (Rev. 4:4, 5:9-10). The number of Levitical courses of priests is identical to the number of elders engaged in worship before God's throne (Rev. 4:10-11). This scene wonderfully pictures the future priestly ministry of the redeemed offering praise, honor, and glory to the Lamb in God's presence forever.

The orders of the priesthood were divided to descendants of Eleazar's *sixteen* sons, and Ithamar's *eight* sons. It is observed that the number *eight*, representing *new beginnings*, and the number *sixteen*, signifying *love*, are key components of being a believer-priest today. Only those who are born again in Christ can serve and worship Him and only those who truly love Him will do so to the best of their ability.

Twenty-Five – Forgiveness of Sins

Although the number *twenty-five* is often connected with larger numbers, especially the number *twenty-five thousand*, it is found by itself 25 times in the Bible (including 3 occurrences of *twenty-fifth*). *Twenty-five* naturally follows *twenty-four* and so does the forgiveness of sin follow the intercession for sin by a mediator, such as a priest. For example, God forgave Israel's offenses and did not destroy them over the golden calf incident and their rebellion at Kadesh Barnea because of Moses' intercession (Ex. 32:30-35, 33:12-17; Num. 14:13-19).

It is interesting that 25 of the 40 times the number *twenty-five* is found in the Bible (this includes compound numbers, e.g., 25,000) it is in the book of Ezekiel and all but two of these occurrences are found in chapters 40 through 48. In this section, the prophet Ezekiel is foretelling a future day when a remnant of His covenant people, the Jews, will be forgiven and finally restored to God in the Promised Land. They will erect a special temple in which to worship God (one that Gentiles cannot enter). Clearly, the number *twenty-five* has significance when the nation of Israel is forgiven and restored to God.

Another illustration of this usage of the number *twenty-five* is contained in Jeremiah's account of Jehoiachin's release from Babylonian prison after 37 years of captivity. This event happened on the *twenty-fifth* day of the twelfth month (Jer. 52:31-34). This king of Judah was not only released from prison, but he was treated with compassion and respect, for *"he ate bread regularly before the king all the days of his life"* (Jer. 52:33).

Being shown mercy by being released from our just punishment is wonderful, but then to receive forgiveness that conveys a high status

(Eph. 2:6) and ensures we experience the riches of God's grace is just incredible (Eph. 1:7). Priestly intercession results in the forgiveness of sin and Christ, as our High Priest and Advocate, is ever making intercession on our behalf (Rom. 8:34; Heb. 7:25; 1 Jn. 2:2). In God's mathematics, the *forgiveness of sin* (*twenty-five*) is the outcome of *five*, symbolizing *grace*, and *twenty* representing *redemption*.

Just as the Levitical priests could not serve in the tabernacle until they were *twenty-five* years old (Num. 8:24), we cannot serve God as believer-priests until our sins have been forgiven.

The Law condemned, but grace came through Christ to offer man the forgiveness of sins. John puts the matter this way: *"And of His fullness we have all received, and grace for grace. For the law was given through Moses, but grace and truth came through Jesus Christ"* (John 1:16-17). Grace upon grace (*five* times *five*) equals *twenty-five*, the forgiveness of sins. The Christian experience is just one wave of God's grace followed by another!

Twenty-Six – Gospel Testimony

The number *twenty-six* is found only once as a standalone number in the Bible (1 Kgs. 16:8). First Kings 16:8 is an historical narrative which does not assist in determining how the number *twenty-six* might be used in a figurative sense.

It has been suggested that the number *twenty-three* may speak of *death*. The number *three* represents *divine completeness and resurrection*. How can death be exchanged for eternal life? The only way is through the gospel of Jesus Christ, which is a possible meaning of the number of *twenty-six*. Jesus Christ is God's Lamb who came to be offered as a sacrifice for the sins of the world, and hence, Christ is spoken of *twenty-six* times in the New Testament as "the Lamb."

Previously, it was observed that the *twenty-third* time that Peter's name occurs in the book of Acts, it was associated with the death of Dorcas (Acts 9:38). Then Peter's name is mentioned *three* more times before he raised Dorcas from the dead (Acts 9:40). *Three* is the number of *resurrection* and Peter raises Dorcas from the dead on the *twenty-sixth* mention of his name in Acts, which is also the third time it is recorded after Dorcas' death. Then, the result of Dorcas' resurrection was that many trusted in the gospel of Jesus Christ (Acts 9:42).

It is noted that this is the only resurrection Peter performs, as recorded in Scripture. What is the only means of exchanging death for resurrection life? The Lord answers this question: *"Most assuredly, I say to you, he who hears My word and believes in Him who sent Me has everlasting life, and shall not come into judgment, but has passed from death into life"* (John 5:24). The *gospel*, or literally "the good news" of Jesus Christ, is represented in the number *twenty-six*.

Interestingly, the *twenty-sixth* time that Noah's name appears in the book of Genesis is when he received *a message of good news* from a dove who had an olive leaf in its mouth (Gen. 8:11). The raven, the unclean bird, brought no such message of hope to Noah (Gen. 8:7). But the dove was a clean bird, a symbol of the Holy Spirit (John 1:32), and thus a message of resurrection life was received – the Earth was alive again. What good news this was for Noah and his family who had been sequestered in an ark with a bunch of smelly animals for over five months. The olive branch is a symbol of peace and the gospel message offers whomsoever will to have peace with God (Rom. 5:1).

Twenty-Seven – Gospel Preaching

The number *twenty-seven* is only found 6 times in Scripture as a standalone number, all of which are either the *twenty-seventh* day or year of something. The first mention of the number may provide a clue to its symbolic meaning. We again return to the story of Noah and his family in the ark:

> *And it came to pass in the six hundred and first year, in the first month, the first day of the month, that the waters were dried up from the Earth; and Noah removed the covering of the ark and looked, and indeed the surface of the ground was dry. And in the second month, on* **the twenty-seventh** *day of the month, the Earth was dried. Then God spoke to Noah, saying, "Go out of the ark, you and your wife, and your sons and your sons' wives with you. Bring out with you every living thing of all flesh that is with you: birds and cattle and every creeping thing that creeps on the Earth, so that they may abound on the Earth, and be fruitful and multiply on the Earth." So Noah went out, and his sons and his wife and his sons' wives with him* (Gen. 8:13-18).

After residing in the ark for over a year, God called them to come out of the ark and to go out into the Earth and be fruitful this happened on the *twenty-seventh* day of the month. This mimics Christ's command to His disciples just prior to His ascension; they were told to go throughout the Earth and proclaim the gospel message (Matt. 28:19-20). They were told to make disciples and to be fruitful. Noah's sons and wives would be fruitful by having children, but the disciples were to share the gospel message so that children of the devil could be born again and become children of God.

Twenty-seven is the sum of the numbers *ten* and *seventeen*. Truly, the only way sinners gain *victory* (*seventeen*) over the condemning testimony of God's *Law* (*ten*) is through hearing and trusting in *the gospel message* (*twenty-seven*). Perhaps this is why the Mercy Seat, which covered the Ark of the Covenant, is mentioned exactly *twenty-seven* times in Scripture. While animal blood on the Mercy Seat secured atonement for sins under the Law, Christ's blood applied in the heavenly sanctuary secured victory over the condemnation of the Law forever!

Twenty-Eight – Eternal Life

Although present in larger numbers 8 times, the number *twenty-eight* stands by itself a mere 5 times in Scripture. The book of Romans seems to provide insight into the metaphorical meaning of the number *twenty-eight*:

> *For if by the one man's offense* [Adam's sin] *death reigned* [twenty-three] *through the one, much more those who receive abundance of grace* [five] *and of the gift of righteousness will reign in life* [twenty-eight] *through the One, Jesus Christ* (Rom. 5:17).

> *Moreover the law entered that the offense might abound. But where sin abounded, grace abounded much more, so that as sin reigned in death* [twenty-three], *even so grace* [five] *might reign through righteousness to eternal life* [twenty-eight] *through Jesus Christ our Lord* (Rom. 5:20-21).

> *For the wages of sin is death* [twenty-three], *but the gift of God* [five] *is eternal life* [twenty-eight] *in Christ Jesus our Lord* (Rom. 6:23).

Paul tells us that grace is the gift God extended to those who trust in Christ as Savior (Rom. 5:15). Paul is saying that the only means of overcoming the *death* (*twenty-three*) we received through Adam is to receive the gift of *grace* (*five*) through Christ – this results in *eternal life* (*twenty-eight*) in Christ. This follows the natural progression of the two previous numbers: *the gospel message* (*twenty-six*), *preaching the gospel message* (*twenty-seven*), and trusting the gospel message result in receiving *eternal life* (*twenty-eight*).

Twice the number *twenty-eight* is tied to the length of the curtains which were combined by loops of blue yarn and gold clasps to create the bottom layer of the four-layered covering of the tabernacle (i.e., the ceiling). There were ten curtains total, but only five curtains were to be connected together by the loops and clasps to create two assembled coverings. One would think that all the curtains should be connected together to create a uniform ceiling, but God intentionally inserted the number *five* into the ceiling design. *Five* is the number of *grace*.

Each linen curtain was four by *twenty-eight* cubits and was to have artistic designs of cherubim woven into the white linen fabric with blue, purple, and scarlet thread (Ex. 26:2-6, 36:8-13). This design was to duplicate God's heavenly abode in His earthly sanctuary. God was taking up residence among men in the newly constructed tabernacle. When an individual trusts Christ, he or she becomes one with Christ and is seated with Him in heavenly places (Eph. 2:6). This speaks of our position in Christ; in Him we have *eternal life and security* forever.

Twenty-Nine – Departure

The number *twenty-nine* is found only 8 times in Scripture. Four times it is associated with the length of reigns of Judean kings. To have any particular name appear at least *twenty-nine* times in Scripture means that individual is a main character in the Bible. The metaphoric meaning of *twenty-nine* is perhaps best discerned by how it is depicted in the lives of key Old Testament characters:

The *twenty-ninth* time that Noah's name appears in Genesis is when God affirms a covenant with Noah, promising to never judge the Earth again by water. After receiving this promise, Noah and his family *departed* the Ark (Gen. 8:9-18).

The *twenty-ninth* time that Abram's name appears in Genesis is when he learned that the Mesopotamian kings had conquered the Jordanian kings (e.g., Sodom and Gomorrah) and had captured his nephew Lot and *departed* the area. Abraham and his armed servants *departed* after them (Gen. 14:14).

The *twenty-ninth* time that Jacob's name appears in Genesis is when his father Isaac sent him away *"and he went to Padan Aram, to Laban,"* his uncle (Gen. 28:5).

The *twenty-ninth* time that Laban's name appears in Genesis is when God commanded Jacob to *depart* from Padan Aram to the land of his father (Gen. 31:2).

The *twenty-ninth* time that Joshua's name is mentioned in Scripture, the Lord commands him, as Israel's new leader, to *"arise, go over this Jordan, you and all this people, to the land which I am giving them"* (Josh. 1:1-2).

The *twenty-ninth* time that Samson's name appears in the book of Judges is when he awoke from sleep to attack the Philistines, but did not know that God had *departed* from him. Samson was consequently captured, blinded, and *led away* into captivity (Judg. 16:20-23).

The *twenty-ninth* time that David's name appears in 1 Samuel is when he *departed* from the safety of Israel's fortifications to battle a giant Philistine named Goliath in the valley Elah below (1 Sam. 17:40-41).

The meaning of *twenty-nine* is difficult to assert, but several Old Testament saints are observed *departing* or *going* somewhere in association with it.

Thirty – Dedication and the Offering of Christ's Blood

The number *thirty* is prevalent throughout Scripture; it appears as a standalone number 82 times in the holy text and is often compounded to create larger numbers. There is a strong connection between the Old and New Testaments as to how the number *thirty* is used, which confirms its symbolic meaning of *dedication,* especially in connection with *the offering of Christ's blood*.

Moses affirmed 7 times in Numbers 4 that priests could not offer sacrifices and apply the blood of the sacrifices in the tabernacle (and later the temple) until they were *thirty* years of age (Num. 4:3, 23, 30, 35, 39, 43, 47). Centuries later, when David divided the priests and Levites into twenty-four orders, he also recognized this age limitation (1 Chron. 23:3). It is noteworthy that David also became the king of Judah at the age of *thirty* (2 Sam. 5:4). He was the first king of Israel that had a heart for God and typified the Greater David to come, the King of kings. A millennium after David, Christ did present Himself to Israel. In keeping

Bible Numbers and Symbols

with these Old Testament patterns, we learn that the Lord Jesus Christ began his earthly ministry at about the same age, *thirty* (Luke 3:23).

When the hour of His sacrifice had come, the Lord Jesus was betrayed by Judas for *thirty* pieces of silver. After feeling guilty for what he had done, Judas returned the money to the temple, but the silver could not be returned to the treasury, because the Pharisees identified it as *"the price of blood" – blood money* (Matt. 26:15, 27:3-6). As previously observed, silver is a symbol of redemption in Scripture and in this instance is clearly being connected with the number *thirty*.

A Levitical priest could not offer blood atonement to God until He was *thirty* years of age. The Lord Jesus began His priestly ministry, as *"the Lamb of God who takes away the sin of the world"* (John 1:29) at the age of *thirty*. He would be both the blood sacrifice offered to God and the offering priest to apply His blood before God for the propitiation of human sin:

> *Being justified freely by His grace through the redemption that is in Christ Jesus, whom God set forth as a propitiation by His blood, through faith, to demonstrate His righteousness, because in His forbearance God had passed over the sins that were previously committed* (Rom. 3:24-25).

> *In Him* [Christ] *we have redemption through His blood, the forgiveness of sins, according to the riches of His grace* (Eph. 1:7).

> *But Christ came as High Priest of the good things to come, with the greater and more perfect tabernacle not made with hands, that is, not of this creation. Not with the blood of goats and calves, but with His own blood He entered the Most Holy Place once for all, having obtained eternal redemption* (Heb. 9:11-12).

The number *ten* represents the testimony of *God's Law* which condemns the sinner. The only solution is for an individual to trust in Christ's work at Calvary and be redeemed by His blood – in this way a repentant sinner has the full offense of his or her sin paid for and is restored to God. *Twenty* is the number for *redemption* and when added to *ten*, we find God's complete solution to sin – *redemption through the offering of Christ's blood*, as represented in the number *thirty*. Thirty represents God's perfect High Priest offering His own blood to redeem what was lost by sin – humanity.

There is an additional picture of this meaning that is embedded in the design of the tabernacle. The eleven goat curtains that formed one of the four layers of the tabernacle ceiling were thirty cubits long (Ex. 26:7-8). Two goats were used during the sixth Feast of Jehovah, called the Day of Atonement, in a vital way to picture what God was accomplishing through His Son at Calvary.

On the Day of Atonement, the High Priest, with his hands on the head of a goat, confessed the sins of the people. This goat, identified as the scapegoat, was then taken out into the wilderness and released; however, a second goat was sacrificed and its blood sprinkled on the mercy seat before God. This symbolized how Christ would suffer and die in the place of the sinner, so that God could righteously remove the judicial penalty of sin from his or her account and impute to him or her a righteous standing. As God has already judged His Son, those who take advantage of Christ's offering by trusting Him as Savior will never experience God's wrath for their sins. Their sin was completely judged once and for all in Christ (Heb. 9:26, 10:10, 12). Thus, on the Day of Atonement, Christ is pictured in both the goat that suffered death for sin, and in the goat which effectively carried away their sins from God's presence.

Samuel was both a prophet and a functioning priest during the time of the Judges; he was Israel's last judge. The *thirtieth* and *thirty-first* times that his name appears in Scripture are connected together. The former reference relates to the people requesting Samuel's intercession before God on their behalf, and the latter, Samuel offers a suckling lamb as a whole burnt offering to the Lord (1 Sam. 7:8-9). Both aspects of an acceptable offering and an acceptable offering priest are connected in this passage and tied with the number *thirty* – it is a lovely reflection of Christ's redemption ministry.

Thirty-One – Offspring

The number *thirty-one* (including *thirty-first*) only occurs 4 times in Scripture and is always used in the literal sense to speak of the reigns of kings or the number of reigning kings. There is really no help here in discerning how the number *thirty-one* may be used in a metaphorical sense in Scripture, so we will investigate various patterns of how the number appears in the Bible.

Bible Numbers and Symbols

It is observed that the *thirty-first* time that Noah's name is found in Genesis we are told the names of his three sons, his *offspring*, and that through them and their wives, God would repopulate the world (Gen. 9:18-19).

The *thirty-first* time that Abraham's name appears in Genesis, we find him praying that God's judgment of *sterility would remove* for Abimelech's clan: *"So Abraham prayed to God; and God healed Abimelech, his wife, and his female servants. Then they bore children"* (Gen. 20:17). Abraham's barren wife Sarah also conceives Isaac, directly after this intercession.

The *thirty-first* time that Isaac's name occurs in Genesis we read that his wife Rebekah, who had been barren for twenty years, *gave birth* to twin boys, Esau and Jacob (Gen. 25:26). This happened directly after Isaac prayed to the Lord to remove Rebekah's barren state.

In all three of these situations, a season of barrenness was endured under God's control, and when His purposes were accomplished, He blessed with children, offspring. The number *thirty-one* seems to be connected with *offspring*, but admittedly its meaning in Scripture is difficult to discern.

Thirty-Two – A Vow, Promise, or Covenant

Although frequently compounded to create larger numbers, *thirty-two* (or *thirty-second*) is found as a standalone number just 10 times in the Bible. It is often employed to speak of a specific timing in the reigns of kings or of the number of kings in a coalition (1 Kgs. 20:1). In looking for patterns as to how the number *thirty-two* may symbolically be applied in the Bible, an indication of a *vow, promise,* or *covenant* does emerge as a strong possibility.

The *thirty-second* time the Abram's name is found in Genesis, God confirms his covenant with Abram. God told Abram not to fear because *"He was his shield and his exceeding great reward"* (Gen. 15:1).

The *thirty-second* time that Jacob's name appears in Genesis, he awakens from his dream of a ladder reaching up to heaven with angels on it and sets up a stone as a pillar and pours oil over it to make his first vow to God (Gen. 28:18-22).

The *thirty-second* time that Moses' name occurs in Exodus, we find him and Aaron confirming God's promise of deliverance from Egyptian bondage to the elders of Israel; this promise was confirmed by miraculous signs (Ex. 4:30).

The *thirty-second* time that David's name is found in 1 Samuel, we find Goliath uttering a curse on David (avowing his death by the power of Goliath's gods; 1 Sam. 17:43).

Nehemiah made a promise to the king to return to Babylon after being in Jerusalem twelve years; he kept that pledge and returned in the *thirty-second* year of Artaxerxes' reign (Neh. 5:14, 13:6).

The figurative meaning of the number *thirty-two* in Scripture is challenging to assert with confidence, but there is some evidence that it is tied to the act of making a declaration of surety, such as a covenant, promise, or vow.

Thirty-Three – Returning or the Hope of Resurrection

The number *thirty-three* occurs 6 times in Scripture and mostly pertains to the reigns of kings. It is also incorporated into the purification process of a Jewish woman after giving birth to a son (Lev. 12:4). While the meaning of this number is elusive, two clues are helpful in suggesting a possible idea associated with the number *thirty-three*.

The *thirty-third* time that Jacob's name emerges in Genesis, we find the patriarch promising to give the Lord a tenth of all that the Lord has given him, that is, if the Lord returned him to the land of his father's house in peace (Gen. 28:20-21). *Thirty-three* is here connected with *returning to his father's house in peace*.

As previously mentioned, the Lord began His three-plus-year ministry at the age of thirty, which means that He was likely crucified, buried, and resurrected from the dead at the age of *thirty-three*. On the morning of His resurrection, the Lord first appeared to Mary Magdalene. After she recognized Him, the Lord told her, *"Do not cling to Me, for I have not yet ascended to My Father; but go to My brethren and say to them, 'I am ascending to My Father and your Father, and to My God and your God'"* (John 20:17).

Later, that same day, the Lord appeared to ten of His disciples who were assembled behind locked doors, for they feared the Jews. The Lord suddenly appeared to them and said: *"Peace be with you"* (John 20:19). Not only did the Lord secure our *peace with God* through His cross (Rom. 5:1), but He also offers us the *peace of God*. This tranquil, settled mind is realized as we align our thinking to His by faith (Phil. 4:7-9).

However, ultimately, believers are destined to experience resurrection and enjoy the utter peace of God's presence forever (2 Pet. 3:12-14).

It is observed that the number *thirty* is associated with the *applying of the blood of Christ* and the number *three* is connected with *resurrection*. The number *thirty-three* would then be the outcome of those who trust in Christ's blood for salvation. This salvation includes the saving of the body through glorification. Our present bodies are not fit for heaven, but in a coming day all the redeemed will be raised up and receive eternal, incorruptible, Christ-like bodies (1 Cor. 15:51-51; Phil. 3:21). The night before His crucifixion the Lord Jesus promised His disciples that He was coming back to get them:

> *In My Father's house are many mansions; if it were not so, I would have told you. I go to prepare a place for you. And if I go and prepare a place for you, I will come again and receive you to Myself; that where I am, there you may be also* (John 14:2-3).

All this to say, there is some evidence in God's Word that the number *thirty-three* may represent *the hopeful return to a place of security* and *the hope of resurrection*. Those experiencing the first resurrection will dwell securely with God forever.

Thirty-Four – Consecration or Naming a Son

The number *thirty-four* is only found once in Scripture by itself and only one other time within a larger compound number. The single reference to *thirty-four* is in Genesis 11:16, *"Eber lived thirty-four years, and begot Peleg."* The named Eber is where the name "Hebrew" is derived from; Abram is the first person identified in the Bible as "the Hebrew" (Gen. 14:13). The meaning of "the Hebrew" is "the passenger," which beautifully encapsulates the pilgrimage of Abram and his strangership in a world. The man naming his son when he was *thirty-four* years of age was marking his descendants as a people who were to be consecrated to God as pilgrims and strangers in the world.

The *thirty-fourth* time Abraham's name occurs in Genesis is directly after he names his newborn son through Sarah, Isaac, as previously commanded. Isaac was then circumcised as required by God in recognition of His covenant with Abraham and his descendants. Isaac was the promised son that Abraham and Sarah had been waiting twenty-five years to arrive. By circumcising Isaac, Abraham was affirming that

Isaac was under God's covenant blessing to him (Gen. 17:9-14). Isaac was named and circumcised in obedience to God's revealed will to ensure all the riches of God's covenant would come upon Isaac. Isaac was consecrated to God; he was sanctified for God's purposes in accomplishing His covenant with Abraham.

A pattern cannot be established by merely two instances of anything. Although the information is limited, it is suggested that the number *thirty-four* may be connected with the idea of *consecration to God*, especially of one's descendants.

Thirty-Five – Hope

As a standalone number, *thirty-five* (including one mention of *thirty-fifth*) occurs a mere 5 times in Scripture. One of these occurrences is found in 2 Chronicles 15:19. Because of King Asa's positive response to the prophet Azariah's message of hope, Judah had an era of peace until the *thirty-fifth* year of his reign. The *thirty-fifth* time that Asa's name is found in Chronicles is in 2 Chronicles 15:2, where Azariah delivers His divine message to the king:

> *Now the Spirit of God came upon Azariah the son of Oded. And he went out to meet Asa, and said to him: "Hear me, Asa, and all Judah and Benjamin.* **The Lord is with you while you are with Him.** *If you seek Him, He will be found by you; but if you forsake Him, He will forsake you. For a long time Israel has been without the true God, without a teaching priest, and without law; but when in their trouble they turned to the Lord God of Israel, and sought Him, He was found by them. And in those times there was no peace to the one who went out, nor to the one who came in, but great turmoil was on all the inhabitants of the lands. So nation was destroyed by nation, and city by city, for God troubled them with every adversity.* **But you, be strong and do not let your hands be weak, for your work shall be rewarded!**" (2 Chron. 15:1-7).

The prophet delivered both a word of exhortation and a wonderful message of hope to King Asa. Sadly, Asa did not continue with the Lord in his latter years on the throne and God's people suffered under his reign.

There is also evidence through Bible mathematics that the number *thirty-five* is connected with the idea of hope. *"And now abide faith, hope, love, these three; but the greatest of these is love"* (1 Cor. 13:3).

The number of *faith* is *nineteen*, and the number of *love* is *sixteen*, and their sum, *thirty-five* produces the last virtue, *hope*.

Paul informs us that our hope is obtained through God's grace: *"Now may our Lord Jesus Christ Himself, and our God and Father, who has loved us and given us everlasting consolation and good hope by grace, comfort your hearts and establish you in every good word and work"* (2 Thess. 2:16). *"That having been justified by His grace we should become heirs according to the hope of eternal life"* (Tit. 3:7). The apostle also states that we can only receive grace through the blood of Christ: *"In Him we have redemption through His blood, the forgiveness of sins, according to the riches of His grace"* (Eph. 1:7). The number of *grace* is *five*, and the number associated with *Christ's blood* is *thirty*; the summation of these two numbers is *thirty-five, hope*. We understand from Scripture that believers now have a future hope because of Christ's blood and God's grace.

Thirty-Six – An Enemy or Adversary

As a standalone number, we observe the number *thirty-six* only twice in our Bibles (Josh. 7:5; 2 Chron. 16:1). We will review both of these references momentarily, but first let us consider evidence in the books of Genesis, Esther, and First Samuel that provide some indication of this number's meaning.

The *thirty-sixth* time that Isaac's name is rendered in Genesis, we have Abimelech, the Philistine governor, confronting him about his deception in posing his wife Rebekah as his sister (Gen. 26:9). As the history of Israel indicates, the Philistines have been and are to this day an enemy of the Jewish people.

Queen Esther invited her husband, King Ahasuerus, and his highest-ranking counterpart, Haman, to a banquet she had prepared (Est. 7). It is during this banquet that she informed King Ahasuerus that there was an evil plot by her enemy to annihilate her and her people. The *thirty-sixth* time that Esther's name appears in the book of Esther is in Esther 7:5, when the king asks her who would presume to do such a thing. She responds, *"The adversary and enemy is this wicked Haman!"* (Est. 7:6). When the queen names the enemy, it is the *thirty-sixth* time that Haman's name is found in the book of Esther. In the book of Esther, the number *thirty-six* is twice connected with the idea of an *enemy* or *adversary*.

The *thirty-sixth* time that we read David's name in 1 Samuel, is when the giant Goliath drew near to meet David, and David, a youth, ran to meet his enemy in battle (1 Sam. 17:48). David had faith in his God to give him victory over the giant. The number for *faith* is *nineteen* and the number of *victory* is *seventeen*. Our adversary's advantage over us is subtracted through faith in the Lord Jesus Christ, who gives us the victory. *"Yet in all these things we are more than conquerors through Him who loved us"* (Rom. 8:37).

There were *thirty-six* Jewish soldiers who were killed during Joshua's first attack on Ai, because there was sin in the camp and the Lord was not with them. Joshua had reasoned that the attack on Jericho had gone so well that only three thousand soldiers would be needed to defeat the smaller city of Ai (Josh. 7:2-5). But facing the enemy in human reasoning and the power of the flesh always results in defeat for God's people. This is the only battle that Israel lost during their seven-year campaign of Canaan; in all, *thirty-six* men were killed by the enemy.

The second, and last, direct reference to the number *thirty-six* is located in 2 Chronicles 16:1: *"In the thirty-sixth year of the reign of Asa, Baasha king of Israel came up against Judah and built Ramah, that he might let none go out or come in to Asa king of Judah."* Again, the number *thirty-six* is connected with a threatening enemy.

Of course, the greatest example of this truth is represented in our salvation, for God achieved victory over sin and death on our behalf through the blood of Christ. Paul tells us the last enemy to be conquered is death (1 Cor. 15:26), which entered the world through Adam's sin (Rom. 5:12). The number for *sin* is *thirteen* and the number of *death* is *twenty-three*; the sum of these two numbers is *thirty-six*, and shows how both sin and death are *the enemies* of the believer.

Thirty-Seven – God's Word

The number *thirty-seven* is found as a standalone number a mere 4 times in Scripture and mainly pertains to Jehoiachin's captivity and the number of David's mighty men. There is not much help here in discerning its meaning, but Genesis 1:1 does offer more information in association with this number: *"In the beginning, God created the heavens and the Earth."* How did God create the heavens and the Earth?

The writer of Hebrews tells us, *"The worlds were framed by the word of God"* (Heb. 11:3). Consequently, we read that God spoke (i.e., "God said") *ten* times during the creation account recorded in Genesis 1. *Ten* is the number of *divine testimony*. The Hebrew text of Genesis 1:1 wonderfully highlights the number *thirty-seven*. Creation happened because God spoke it into being, hence *thirty-seven* is associated with *God's Word* – a perfect testimony of Himself.

Let us begin by examining the first two of the seven Hebrew words in Genesis 1:1. Please note that the Hebrew text reads right to left. The first word *Breeshiyt*, rendered "in the beginning" has a Hebrew numerical value of 913 and *Elohiym* (*Elohim*) translated "God" has a value of 86. The sum of these two numbers is 999, which is also equal to *thirty-seven* times *three* cubed ($999 = 37 \times 3^3$). Three is a perfect prime number.

     86   913

בראשית ברא אלהים את השמים ואת הארץ

    God In the beginning

The second, fourth and fifth Hebrew words in Genesis 1:1 also have a numerical value of 999 and thus the same breakdown ($999 = 37 \times 3^3$).

   395 401   203

בראשית ברא אלהים את השמים ואת הארץ

  the heavens created

The third, fifth, and sixth Hebrew words in Genesis 1:1 have a numerical value of 777, which is also divisible by *three*, *seven*, and *thirty-seven*. All these numbers are prime numbers, but *three* and *seven* are perfect prime numbers (i.e., each represents some aspect of God's perfection).

   296   395   86

בראשית ברא אלהים את השמים ואת הארץ

 the earth the heavens God

The Hebrew letters producing our English rendering, *"In the beginning God"* total up to 999, which is equal to *thirty-seven* times *three* cubed. As the number *three* represents divine completeness and resurrection, cubing this number amplifies its meaning. God is perfect in all His ways and all that He that says is perfect too. What He says will happen and be completely good. God says *seven* times in Genesis 1 that what He had spoken into existence was "good" – all that had happened fully met all of His expectations.

Interestingly, the Greek word for Jesus in the New Testament is *Iesous*. The numerical total of the six Greek letters composing the Lord's given name is 888 (I =10, E=8, S=200, O=70, U=400, S=200), which is also divisible by *thirty-seven*, *twenty-four* times. *Twenty-four* is the number of *the priesthood* in Scripture. Accordingly, Jesus Christ is referred to as "the Word" that was God from the beginning (John 1:1-2). This living Word spoke into existence all that exists (John 1:4). The Word became flesh and dwelt among men (John 1:14). Furthermore, the writer of Hebrews tells us that God spoke to us by sending us His Son (His Word) into the world:

> *God, who at various times and in various ways spoke in time past to the fathers by the prophets, has in these last days spoken to us by His Son, whom He has appointed heir of all things, through whom also He made the worlds; who being the brightness of His glory and the express image of His person, and upholding all things by the word of His power, when He had by Himself purged our sins, sat down at the right hand of the Majesty on high* (Heb. 1:1-3).

The Lord Jesus Christ was able to purge our sins, because He willingly offered His life as a perfect sacrifice for us and then as High Priest offered up His own blood to God for the propitiation for our sin. The number *twenty-four* is the number for the *priesthood* and Christ is our Great High Priest who has secured our salvation forever (Heb. 2:17, 3:1, 4:14, 5:10, 6:20, 7:26, 8:1, 9:11, 25, 10:21). The Lord's own name represents Him as God's Living Word to us (*thirty-seven*) and our Great High Priest (*twenty-four*).

Thirty-Eight – Bondage

The number *thirty-eight* is compounded twice to created larger numbers in the Old Testament; it is found by itself only three times in the Old Testament and once in the New Testament. In Deuteronomy 2:14 the number is used to speak of the *thirty-eight*-year interval in which the Israelites wandered in the wilderness under judgment for their rebellion at Kadesh Barnea. During this time those twenty years old and older were bound to a death sentence, excluding Caleb and Joshua.

Bible Numbers and Symbols

In 1 Kings 16:29, Ahab became king of Israel in the *thirty-eighth* year of King Asa's reign in Judah. Ahab put the Northern Kingdom in the bondage of gross idolatry; he was more wicked than any king in Israel previously. Many Jehovah-worshipers were put to death during his reign.

We read in John 5:5 of a man who suffered from an infirmity which practically immobilized him for *thirty-eight* years. The Lord released him from the bondage of his condition by saying, *"Rise, take up your bed and walk"* and the man did just that (John 5:8).

The *thirty-eighth* time that Abram's name appears in Genesis, he is making God aware that because He has given him no son, the heir of his house will be Eliezer, his *servant* from Damascus (Gen. 15:3).

The thirty-eighth time Abraham's name appears in Genesis, Ishmael, the son of the bondwoman, was mocking little Isaac and Sarah requested that Hagar and Ishmael be cast out of the family clan (Gen. 21:9-10). There is not a lot of information pertaining to the number *thirty-eight* in the Bible, but the idea of *bondage* in one form or another seems to be connected with it.

Thirty-Nine – Sorrow and Suffering

The number *thirty-nine* is compounded to create a larger number once and stands by itself only thrice in the Bible; all occurrences are in the Old Testament. Two references related to when two kings of Israel began their reigns as marked by the *thirty-ninth* year of rule of two kings of Judah. The two kings of Israel that are referenced, Shallum and Menahem, did evil in the sight of the Lord (2 Kgs. 15:13-22). Menahem murdered Shallum to become king and then he attacked Tiphsah in his territory and ripped open all the pregnant women in retaliation for their lack of surrender. The Assyrians also levied a burdensome tax on the Jews during Menahem's reign.

The third reference speaks of King Asa of Judah becoming severely diseased in his feet in the *thirty-ninth* year of his reign. Asa was a good king who followed the Lord early on, but in his latter years he oppressed some of the people and did not seek the Lord (2 Chron. 16:12). As this is the only unusual feature tied with the number *thirty-nine*, the number may symbolize *disease*.

There are two more circumstances in the Bible that are marked by the number *thirty-nine*. The first relates to the reign of King Josiah. Josiah and Hezekiah were Judah's most righteous kings after the

Biblical Numbers

kingdom split (i.e., after Solomon's death). Josiah was eight years old when he began to reign in 640 B.C. (2 Kgs. 22:1). He most likely died at the age of *thirty-nine*, while trying to prevent the Egyptian army from passing through Israel to war with Babylon (2 Chron. 35:20-27). The Babylonian Chronicles place the battle of Harran, where the combined forces of Assyria and Egypt fought against Babylon and lost, in August-September 609 B.C. King Josiah probably died about a month before this battle occurred. This was a most sorrowful time for the Jewish people. They had been blessed and experienced revival under Josiah, but the remaining kings of Judah were all wicked men who caused them much harm.

A common punishment under the Law and practiced in both the Old and New Testaments was that of scourging (Lev. 19:20). According to Deuteronomy 25:1-3, up to forty stripes could be administered, but to ensure compliance with the Law, the Jews limited themselves to "forty stripes minus one" or *thirty-nine* stripes (2 Cor. 11:24).

The biblical information pertaining to the number *thirty-nine* is minimal; however, in each of the five instances discussed above, there is an idea of *sorrow and suffering* present.

Forty – Probation and Testing

Of the 162 times the number *forty* is found in Scripture, it is only compounded to create larger numbers 58 times (including all the references to numbers in the Bible between *forty* and *fifty*). This observation would indicate that the number *forty* does have a significant meaning in Scripture beyond its mathematical quantity.

From a mathematical point of view, *forty* is the product of *four* (*earthly order*) and *ten* (*divine testimony*). The idea being that God has revealed a particular truth and Earthlings are accountable to obey it. Both this analysis and the way the number *forty* is used dozens of times in Scripture convey the idea of a *probationary test or trial*. *Forty* is often the duration that God tests the obedience of His people before passing judgment upon them, if found guilty.

Moses lived in Egypt for *forty* years, then was morally refined in the wilderness of Midian for *forty* years, before leading the Israelites out of Egypt and into the wilderness for another *forty* years. There were also three occasions in which Moses was on Mount Sinai in God's presence *forty* days and nights (Ex. 24:18, 34:1-28; Deut. 8:18). At Kadesh

Barnea, Moses sent twelve Jewish spies into Canaan for *forty* days, to investigate the land God had promised them (Num. 13:25, 14:34).

The Bible records a few occasions when individuals went *forty* days without food or drink through the supernatural care of God: Elijah during his wilderness experience (1 Kgs. 19:8), Moses before Jehovah on Mount Horeb (Ex. 34:28), and Christ during His testing in the wilderness while He fasted (Matt. 4:1-11; Mark 1:13). After His resurrection, the Lord also appeared to encourage and commission His disciples over a *forty*-day period before ascending into heaven (Acts 1:1-11).

The number *forty* is used in Scripture to represent *probation* and *testing*, which explains its frequent occurrence. At times, God extended the nation of Israel *forty*-year probationary periods to test or prove them: the Israelites were tested in the wilderness *forty* years (Deut. 8:2-5), delivered and had rest during the *forty* years that Othniel, Barak, and Gideon judged Israel (Judg. 3:11, 5:31, 8:28). Five Jewish kings had *forty*-year reigns over God's covenant people: David, Solomon, Jeroboam, Jehoash, and Joash (2 Sam. 5:4; 1 Kgs. 11:42; 2 Kgs. 12:17, 12:1; 2 Chron. 24:1). Another demonstration of *forty* as the number of probation and testing is found in God's dealings with Nineveh; the prophet Jonah preached that, unless the inhabitants repented, God's judgment would fall on them in *forty* days (Jon. 3:4).

The first time Moses spent *forty* days on Mount Sinai served not only as an opportunity for him to receive the Law, but was also a time of testing for the Israelites: would they be faithful to their newly-affirmed covenant with Jehovah? They failed the test (they crafted and worshiped a golden calf) and were judged. However, the second time Moses was before the Lord for *forty* days, the Israelites remained repentant and faithful. They patiently waited for Moses (the only one who could make intercession for them) to descend the mountain and tell them whether or not they had been forgiven.

When Moses did return, with God's covenant in hand, the news was most welcome – God had pardoned their transgressions, He would remain among them, and He would go with them to the Promised Land. The Israelites had come to realize that life has no meaning unless God is at the center of it. Whether that be for *forty* seconds or *forty* days or *forty* years, every believer will experience seasons of probation and testing.

Other Unique Numbers

While numbers one through forty in the Bible appear to have distinct symbolic meanings above their mathematical value, there are also a few numbers above forty which offer figurative significance. This understanding permits deeper insight into the prophetic or typological context of the associated passage. Here are a few examples.

Seventy – The Jewish Nation of Israel

The number *seventy* is especially associated with the nation of Israel throughout Scripture (Ex. 1:5). Genesis 46 provides the first roster of the nation, which includes the names of those in Jacob's family who traveled with him to Egypt. In all, twelve sons, fifty-three grandsons, four great-grandsons, one daughter Dinah, and one granddaughter Serah are named.

Although Jacob had four wives, other daughters and granddaughters (Gen. 46:7) they are not included in this number, nor were his son's wives or grandson's wives. As women were not included in any Israelite census, it seems likely that Dinah and Serah are only mentioned as substitutes for the two sons of Judah, Er and Onan, who were judged by God in Canaan. This gave a count of sixty-six and hence, preserved the symbolism of *seventy* as representing Israel. Counting Joseph and his two sons, who were already in Egypt, and Jacob himself, the total number of persons composing the nation of Israel at this time was stated to be *seventy*, but clearly there were dozens of females beyond this figure (Gen. 46:5).

Later, God appointed seventy elders to shepherd His people for centuries to come (Num. 11:16). During New Testament times, there were seventy members of the Sanhedrin and seventy witnesses sent out into Judea by Christ (Luke 10:1). This connection between the number *seventy* and the nation of Israel can also be seen in the books of Jeremiah and Daniel where it relates to the regathering of the Jewish people to their homeland (i.e., in the seventieth week; Dan. 9:24-27).

One Hundred Twenty-Seven – Israel's Rejection of Christ and Resulting Blindness

It is quite significant that Sarah is the only woman in all of Scripture whose age at the time of her death is recorded, 127 years. Sarah's age at death allows us to determine Isaac's corresponding age when this tragic event took place; he was 37 years old.

Abraham was a stranger in the land (Gen. 23:4); he held no legal title to the land upon which he dwelled to lawfully bury his wife. Therefore, he asked the children of Heth for a piece of property to bury his wife's body, namely the cave of Machpelah near Hebron (Gen. 23:19). The price of the property was agreed to, and Abraham purchased it and buried his deceased wife. She was the first of the patriarchal family to die in the Promised Land. Her burial in Canaan and not their homeland would serve as a declaration to the inhabitants of Canaan and to their descendants that the land upon which they lived and died was truly their home forever.

Genesis 21 through 25 are strongly linked together to foreshadow the prophetic fulfillment of Christ's first and second advents to the Earth. Accordingly, these chapters closely parallel the prophetic content contained in the Kingdom parables of Matthew 13. These seven parables bridge the gap between the First Advent of the Lord to Earth to become a man to suffer for sin and His Second Advent in which His kingdom will be established and all that is evil and wicked will be removed. The "kingdom of God" was foretold in the Old Testament, announced by John the Baptist and Jesus, and rejected by the Jews. The kingdom was then spiritually offered to the Gentiles in the interim before it will be physically established on Earth and, in the finale, become the eternal state of the new heaven and new Earth. All this is shown in chronological order in Genesis 21 through 25.

In Genesis 21, we have the birth of the promised son – the only begotten son of Abraham (Heb. 11:17), which pictures Christ's birth. In Genesis 22, the offering of the son by the father is observed, which foreshadows Calvary. Genesis 23 records the death and burial of Sarah. These events speak of the rejection of Jesus the Messiah by the Jews, their subsequent disciplinary "blindness" (Rom. 11:7), and that, as a nation, they are a treasure reburied in the purchased field (Matt. 13:44). In Genesis 24, the Holy Spirit is introduced to us in type as the servant of Abraham who traveled out of the land of Israel to woo a bride for the father's son. The Holy Spirit is presently wooing a Gentile bride for the Lord Jesus. Genesis 24 concludes with the bride and the groom meeting for the first time (picturing the rapture of the church), and both returning to his father's home (heaven) where the bride is loved and cherished forever. Genesis 25 records that Abraham took another wife (Keturah). In seed form, Abraham's marriage to Keturah typifies the future restoration of the adulterous and divorced wife of Jehovah – Israel (Jer. 3:8; Ezek. 16; Hosea 2:14-23). The climax of Abraham's life is in Genesis 25:5 when the son, with his new bride, inherits all things. This, of course, pictures the Lord Jesus establishing His kingdom on Earth with His bride, the Church, who will rule and reign with Him (Matt. 20:20-28; 2 Tim. 2:12; Rev. 4:4).

Let us refocus now on the content of Genesis 23. Through the "Kingdom Parables," the Lord Jesus was foretelling that the Jews, who had already been scattered and lost among the nations for 600 years for committing spiritual adultery (Ezek. 36:16-25), would be nationally found for the purpose of offering Himself as their King. They would reject Him and, thus, continue to be lost among the nations until their repentance during the last days of the Tribulation Period. In order to be able to retrieve them from the nations later and to restore them as His people, the Lord first had to pay the debt of their sin at Calvary. In the fifth of the Kingdom Parables, Christ alludes to this: *"Again, the kingdom of heaven is like treasure hidden in a field, which a man found and hid; and for joy over it he goes and sells all that he has and buys that field"* (Matt. 13:44). Just as Abraham bought the field for a price and would hide Sarah in it, God the Father would purchase Israel through the blood of His own Son and leave them hidden in the world until their restoration.

There is a brief hint of Israel's physical and spiritual resurrection in the narrative in Genesis 23:3: *"Abraham stood up from before his dead."* Ezekiel describes this national wonder in chapter 37 of his book. In a vision, he describes a valley of dry bones before him that pictures the nation of Israel dead in the world. God instructs Ezekiel to prophesy upon these dry bones. As he does, the bones begin to assemble themselves into full human skeletal structures. After 2600 years of Gentile rule, Israel became a political reality in May 1948, even though the nation still remains dead in a spiritual sense. As Ezekiel preached, the skeletons took on flesh – this great army had the appearance of life, but in fact there was no life within them.

This event coincides with the fig tree (religious Israel) shooting forth her fig leaves before summer (before the Tribulation Period) in Matthew 24. There are leaves upon the tree, depicting a religious reality (the Jews will be sacrificing again), but there is no spiritual fruit. Spiritual fruit can only come through spiritual rebirth. The nation of Israel will not experience spiritual rebirth until the end of the Tribulation Period. During the Tribulation Period, the Jews will be offering sacrifices again under the Levitical system. Before the Anti-Christ can stop these sacrifices during the middle of the Tribulation Period, they must begin again (Matt. 24:15, 2 Thess. 2:4-6). Finally, at the end of the Tribulation Period, the Jews will receive the Holy Spirit and obtain spiritual life in Christ. This is illustrated in the vision when Ezekiel prophesies to the wind (speaking of the Holy Spirit in type) to come and give life and breath upon the great army. There is a yet future resurrection of the hidden treasure – the nation of Israel unto spiritual and eternal life.

Sarah, who pictures Israel (e.g., Israel is the woman who bore the only begotten son in Rev. 12:1-2), was buried in the cave of Machpelah near Hebron. The Hebrew root word for "Hebron" comes from *cheber*, which means "a society or a fellowship." The Hebrew root word for "Machpelah" is derived from *kaphal*, which means "to fold together," or by implication, "to repeat" or "to double." Exodus 19:5 and Psalm 135:4 inform us that God considers Israel "a treasure" unto Himself. It seems, then, that what is pictured here in Sarah's death is Israel being cut off from God because of their rejection of God's Son. This occurred after the offering of the Son (Christ's first advent), but before the wooing of a Gentile bride for the Son after Christ's resurrection. A "society" and a "treasure" were, thus, hidden again in the world, a second time or a "double" time. However, at the Lord's second coming to the Earth, He will be accepted by the Jewish nation (Zech. 12:10), and they will then receive the Holy Spirit and be restored unto God as His people. The hidden treasure that Christ previously paid for at Calvary will be restored to Him forever. The events surrounding Sarah's death, the fact that she was buried in a cave, that the cave was called Machpelah and was near Hebron convey a prophetic portrait of God's future dealing with the nation of Israel.

When Sarah died, the marriage covenant with Abraham was severed (Rom. 7:1-6); this event was followed by a marriage covenant instituted in Genesis 24 between Isaac and Rebekah, thus portraying the New Covenant in Christ's blood, which put away the Old Covenant. Isaac was comforted concerning his mother's death when he married Rebekah three years later. The Lord Jesus declared the Kingdom gospel message to the nation of Israel for approximately three years before the Jews rejected and crucified Him. He was comforted over Israel's rejection shorting after His resurrection by being married to a Gentile bride, called the Church. The record of Sarah's age at the time of her death enables us to identify the typological projection of Sarah, Isaac, and Rebekah in Genesis 23 to that of God's dealings with Israel and the Church in relationship to Christ.

The death of Sarah naturally permits Abraham to receive a new wife in Genesis 25 (Keturah). This marriage occurs after Isaac is joined to Rebekah. The marriage with Keturah, who bears Abraham six sons, depicts the future restoration of a refined and fruitful Israel (Abraham's seed) with Jehovah. Obviously, the resurrection of Sarah to picture this event would have been beyond the natural implications of the narrative.

Refined Israel will be restored to God after the Church Age ends (i.e., the Church will be in heaven with Christ during the Tribulation Period). Accordingly, Isaac and Rebekah were joined together in Genesis 24 prior to Abraham's marriage to Keturah. The Old Covenant had its strength in the Law, which could not be kept and, thus, brought death, but the New Covenant is empowered by God's grace through Christ's blood. As a result, the New Covenant established by Christ, brought salvation to both Jew and Gentile (Luke 22:20; Eph. 3:6-7).

One Hundred Fifty-Three – Abundant Blessing

The meaning of the number *one hundred fifty-three* is associated with a miraculous catch of fish near the shore of the Sea of Galilee (John 21:1-11). Shortly after Christ's resurrection, the disciples journeyed to Galilee as requested by the Lord. While waiting for further instructions, some of the disciples had either become restless, and at Peter's suggestion went fishing. But after an exhausting night of fishing, they had nothing to show for their effort.

Early the next morning, a man on the shore called out to the disciples who were still in their boat and asked them if they had caught anything. The disciples did not know it was the Lord Jesus at this juncture. After affirming that they had caught nothing, the Lord told them to drop their net on the right side of the boat. The disciples complied and they soon found out that they could not pull the net back into the boat because it full of fish. John then recognized that the man speaking to them was their Lord and announced that fact to the other disciples. The net full of fished had to be dragged to the shore in order to retrieve the vast quantity of fish; when counted there were *153* fish. The disciples, many of whom were previous fisherman, were surprised that the net remained intact and that some of the fish were not lost. The number *153* then testifies to the abundant blessings of God to us, which under His control cannot be thwarted by natural or demonic opposition.

Interestingly, when *three*, the number of divine essence and *twelve*, the number of divine administration, are both squared and then added together, their sum is *153* ($3^2 + 12^2 = 153$). Our eternal blessings in Christ are ensured by the power of our triune God.

About three years earlier the Lord had provided Peter, Andrew, James and John another miraculous catch of fish after a night of catching nothing. But in that situation, Peter had merely let down one net after the Lord told him to lower his nets (Luke 5:4-5). As a result of incomplete obedience, some of the blessing that could have been theirs was lost. This is a good reminder that without Christ we can do nothing (John 15:5); and we dare not call Him Lord if we are not willing to do what He says (Luke 6:46). God longs to bless His children, but He also expects obedience from those who are His.

Two Hundred Seventy-Six – Sovereign Control

In Acts 27, we read of a terrible Mediterranean storm that threatened the lives of Paul and everyone else sailing with him to Rome. Because the violent storm had lasted for many days most of the *276* passengers, many of which were prisoners, were in great despair. Paul was told by an angel that though the ship would be broken up, no lives would be lost if they remained in the ship until they were cast safely on an island.

As previously mentioned, the number *twenty-three* represents *death* and the number *twelve*, God's *perfect administration* in Scripture. *Two hundred seventy-six* divided by the number of *death*, *twenty-three*, is exactly *twelve*. Hence, God was showing His sovereign control over life and death in this matter and He had chosen to save all of the ship's complement from the storm to demonstrate His authority and power to them.

Obviously, one occurrence does not provide sufficient information to establish a pattern as to what a particular number may mean. But in this unique situation, the number *276* is tied to God's sovereign authority. May we be encouraged that there is no situation that is beyond God's control and He is able to save to the uttermost!

Six Hundred Sixty-Six – The Number of the Antichrist

We read in 2 Chronicles 9, that in addition to the gold Solomon obtained through trade taxes and tolls, he received 666 talents in annual revenue from subservient nations under his rule (2 Chron. 9:13). The governors of these lands and even the kings of Arabia brought gold and silver to Solomon (2 Chron. 9:14). Out of these resources King Solomon fashioned a impressive throne of ivory and overlaid it with pure gold (2 Chron. 9:17). This golden throne had an attached footstool and *six* steps with a guardian lion on either side of each step and two more lions – one under each of two armrests (2 Chron. 9:18-19). The writer affirms that no other kingdom had ever had a throne matching the grandeur of Solomon's throne. The number *six* represents man's doings apart from God, and Solomon's throne containing *six* stairs, though glorious, was not to last. Regrettably, we read that Solomon's foreign wives (who he was prohibited from marrying) eventually turned his heart from following the Lord (1 Kgs. 11:1-8).

The only other reference to the number *666* in Scripture is in its association with the Antichrist during the Tribulation Period. At that time, he will establish a throne even greater than Solomon's and He will rule over all the nations and control the world's wealth. *Six* is the *number of man* and *three* the number of *unity*.

John identifies three beasts in Revelation chapters 12 and 13 which form the unholy trinity:

- A terrible red dragon having seven heads, ten horns, and seven crowns (one for each of its heads) is used to represent Satan (Rev. 12:3). He is identified as Satan, the devil, and the serpent of old (Rev. 12:9).

- A beast rising up out of the sea (i.e., the nations), with seven heads and ten horns on one head with each horn having a crown represents the Antichrist who speaks for the dragon (Rev. 13:1, 17:9-14).

- A beast coming up out of the land (i.e., Israel) and having two horns, like a lamb, represents the false prophet who talks like the dragon (Rev. 13:11).

Bible Numbers and Symbols

    These beasts form an unholy trio that clearly mocks the Holy Trinity in form and operation: God the Father directs, the Son does the Father's will, and the Holy Spirit enables the Son to do the Father's will. Satan directs the affairs of the unholy trio. The Antichrist is the devil's human representative on the Earth and does his will. The false prophet gives honor to the beast through miracles and deceives many into worshiping the beast, and thus honoring Satan (Rev. 13:14-15). These similarities between the unholy trio and the Holy Trinity are profound.

    The mark of the beast, *666*, is man's number, *six*, threefold. During the Tribulation Period, man will largely be in cahoots with the unholy trinity to rebel against the true Triune God. No doubt the latest feats in human technology will be combined with satanic authority to achieve fiendish control of the world's political and economic systems. Those rejecting the mark of the beast will not be able to buy or sell goods and if caught, will be put to death. The good news is that many will choose to be beheaded by the Antichrist (Rev. 20:4) rather than take his mark of identification and worship him (Rev. 7:9-14).

Biblical Metaphor

The Lord Jesus realized the benefit of metaphor and allegory and often incorporated those forms of language into His sermons. For example, He proclaimed to His audience that He was "the Bread of Life," "the Light of the World," "the Good Shepherd," "the Way," "the Truth," the Life," and "the Vine." If anyone was spiritually hungry or thirsty, they would find satisfaction by coming to Him. The Lord offered to illuminate the way to God for those weary of wandering in satanic darkness. He promised to sacrificially care for those who came to Him and to supply each person what was necessary to enjoy a productive and blessed life in Him. The use of such figurative language assists us in understanding the ideas being conveyed.

Accordingly, our all-wise and gracious God often includes symbolic or allegorical information while communicating to us through the plain language of the biblical narrative. We can appreciate this multifaceted form of expression because He assigns consistent figurative meanings to various numbers, materials, elements, creatures, colors, etc. in Scripture. Let us investigate this emblematic means of communication through biblical metaphor besides that which is found in numerical expression.

The following examples are organized into six categories: Heavenly Creatures, Earthly Creatures in Sacrifice, Other Earthly Creatures, Metals and Materials, Colors, and Miscellaneous.

Heavenly Creatures

Paul states, that God has clearly shown Himself to all men through His creation (Rom. 1:20). Accordingly, all creation, visible or invisible, provides a wonderful testimony of God's greatness: *"Bless the Lord, all His works, in all places of His dominion. Bless the Lord, O my soul!"* (Ps. 103:22). Included in *"all places of His dominion"* are spiritual beings in heavenly realms, which continually declare the glory of God and praise His name (Ps. 103:20).

Cherubim

The scriptural accounts of the cherubim in Ezekiel 1 and 10 disclose that these beings each have four faces: the face of a lion, the face of an ox, the face of a man, and the face of an eagle. The faces of these beings reflect the same glories of the Lord Jesus that are presented in the main themes of each Gospel. The *lion* is the king of the beasts, which reflects Matthew's perspective of Christ the King. The *ox*, as a beast of burden, is harnessed for the rigors of serving, and pictures Mark's presentation of Christ the Servant. The face of the *man* clearly agrees with Luke's prevalent theme of the Lord's humanity. Lastly, the *eagle* flies high above all the other creatures; the divine essence of the Savior is in view here as it is in John's gospel.

What is not a reflective glory of Christ in these heavenly creatures is not described to us, but is rather willfully covered by their own wings. No competing glories will be tolerated in God's presence – only His glory is to be seen and appreciated.

The Cherubim, the guardians of God's throne, were given four wings, but only use two for the activity of flying or for shielding God's shekinah glory (Ezek. 1:5-11, 10:1-5). As demonstrated in the design of the Mercy Seat that covered the Ark of the Covenant, two Cherubim used two of their wings to cover their own intrinsic glories and two to covered the Mercy Seat (Ex. 25:18-22). God, dwelling between the Cherubim and above the Mercy Seat, could then talk to Moses safely in the Most Holy Place of the tabernacle.

Seraphim

The Seraphim, who vocally praise the holiness of God in heaven, have six wings, but only use two for flying (Isa. 6:2-3). Their other four wings are used to cover their faces and feet in God's presence. The seraphim have one face each.

The four living creatures who praise God as they flying above His throne (Rev. 4:6-9) are likely Seraphim, but it is possible that they are four unique creatures who have similar occupations at the Seraphim. The four living creatures each have one face; each has one of the four faces of the cherubim to again reflect the fourfold gospel presentation of Christ to humanity. They have eyes within and around to visually reflect the omniscience of their Creator.

Faces of Heavenly Creatures Summary
Lion – Royalty, Nobility
Ox – Service, Humility
Man – Humanity
Eagle – Deity, Supremacy

Earthly Creatures in Sacrifice

God uses various earthly creatures in Scripture to represent important aspects of His Son's character and attributes or to portray His redemptive ministry. The fact that God limits the representation to only a select few creatures, would suggest that He has very specific ideas that He wants us to understand about Christ.

For example, in the Levitical sacrifices, we observe that there were only four animals and two kinds of birds to be offered: oxen and cattle were taken from the herd, sheep and goats from the flock, while turtle doves and pigeons represented the fowls. Each of these creatures had a "clean" designation and a particular and unique representation of Christ's personage, attributes, or ministry.

Oxen or Cattle – Service, Humility

The offering of the herd included oxen or cattle. Only a male, a bull, was permitted for the burnt offering and some sin offerings. Oxen and cattle were yoked to pull farm implements, sleds, carts, wagons, etc. Oxen, especially, were beasts of burden and thus represent Christ as the lowly servant of Jehovah. This vantage point is further brought to light in Mark's gospel, which shows the Lord quickly traveling from one place to another to provide continuous service to others without thought of Himself:

> *Yet it shall not be so among you; but whoever desires to become great among you shall be your servant. And whoever of you desires to be first shall be slave of all. For even the Son of Man did not come to be served, but to serve, and to give His life a ransom for many* (Mark 10:43-45).

The Lord's meek and humble character, His compassion for the suffering, and His resolute spirit in the face of opposition invite us to follow His example – He was a true Servant of God. Mark's perspective of Christ's selfless ministry shows us that true love needs no title to serve, just the power to do so, which is supplied by Him alone.

Sheep – Meekness

In Scripture, sheep are known for their tendency to go their own way and to become lost (Luke 15:4). Isaiah compares this propensity to the nature of fallen humanity; each of us proves our inherent depravity by going our own way and not following after God (Isa. 53:6; 1 Pet. 2:25). Yet, this natural tendency is contrasted with the Lord's perfect sinless behavior, who as the Lamb of God always did the Father's will (John 5:30). Sheep are defenseless creatures; it is likely this disposition of meekness and lowliness that the Spirit of God desires us to appreciate about the Lord Jesus:

> *He was oppressed and He was afflicted, yet He opened not His mouth; He was led as a lamb to the slaughter, and as a sheep before its shearers is silent, so He opened not His mouth* (Isa. 53:7).

> *Who, when He was reviled, did not revile in return; when He suffered, He did not threaten, but committed Himself to Him who judges righteously* (1 Pet. 2:23).

The Lord Jesus did not try to defend Himself when arrested. He did not resist His accusers, but rather submitted to and endured their mockery and cruelty, though He had the wherewithal to deliver Himself from it.

The Goat – Evil, Sin

Goats were used to symbolize evil in the Bible. For example, those who align with the Antichrist during the Tribulation Period are referred to as goats when the Lord judges the nations; unlike His "sheep," these individuals are condemned and not permitted to enjoy Christ's millennial kingdom (Matt. 25:33,41). At Calvary, the Lord Jesus Christ, who knew no sin, took our sin upon Himself; He became sin for us:

> *For He made Him who knew no sin to be sin for us, that we might become the righteousness of God in Him* (2 Cor. 5:21).

> *Who Himself bore our sins in His own body on the tree, that we, having died to sins, might live for righteousness – by whose stripes you were healed* (1 Pet. 2:24).

On the Day of Atonement, the High Priest, with his hands on the head of a goat, confessed the sins of the people. This goat, identified as the scapegoat, was then taken out into the wilderness and released; however, a second goat was sacrificed and its blood sprinkled on the mercy seat before God. This symbolized how Christ would suffer and die in the place of the sinner, so that God could righteously remove the judicial penalty of sin from his or her account and impute to him or her a righteous standing.

As God has already judged His Son, those who take advantage of Christ's offering by trusting Him as Savior will never experience God's wrath for their sins. Their sin was completely judged once and for all in Christ (Heb. 9:26, 10:10, 12). Thus, on the Day of Atonement, Christ is pictured in both the goat that suffered death for sin, and in the goat which effectively carried away their sins from God's presence.

The Turtledove – Mourning, Sorrow

The turtledove may represent mourning in Scripture (Isa. 38:14, 59:11). The Lord Jesus was grieved over Israel's rejection of Himself as their Messiah and this is symbolized by the turtledove.

> *O Jerusalem, Jerusalem, the one who kills the prophets and stones those who are sent to her! How often I wanted to gather your children together, as a hen gathers her chicks under her wings, but you were not willing! See! Your house is left to you desolate* (Matt. 23:37-38).
>
> *He came to His own, and His own did not receive Him* (John 1:11).

When the Son withdrew from the dimensionless and timeless realm of majesty on high to descend to the Earth, He willingly placed Himself under creation order and the rule of fallen humanity. It is one thing to suffer for your own bad behavior; it is quite another to suffer and die in the place of another when you have not done anything wrong. And a grander mystery yet is what compelled the Lord to willingly die for those who did not in the slightest degree appreciate His sacrifice.

The Pigeon – Innocence, Gentleness

The pigeon may symbolize the innocence and gentleness of the Lord Jesus (Matt. 10:16). He blessed little children, healed the sick, freed those who were demonically possessed, and tirelessly taught the masses the way of life. It is also worth noting that birds were primarily a poor man's offering, and this corresponds to the poverty Christ took upon Himself when He entered this world:

> *And Jesus said to him, "Foxes have holes and birds of the air have nests, but the Son of Man has nowhere to lay His head"* (Matt. 8:20).

> *For you know the grace of our Lord Jesus Christ, that though He was rich, yet for your sakes He became poor, that you through His poverty might become rich* (2 Cor. 8:9).

The Lord Jesus ventured from the glories of heaven to be incarnated in the womb of a virgin and then to be born into a poor family (Luke 1:34, 2:24). He then lived as a lowly stranger, the Messenger of God among the very hostile creatures He had created and was laboring to save.

Earthly Creature in Sacrifice Summary
Ox – Service, Humility
Sheep – Meekness
Goat – Evil, Sin
Turtledove – Mourning, Sorrow
Pigeon – Innocence, Gentleness

Other Earthly Creatures

Besides the heavenly beings, and the clean animals and birds offered in Levitical sacrifices there are many other creatures which are assigned a figurative idea in Scripture. For example, the book of Proverbs highlights the diligent behavior of the ant as good example for us to follow in life (Prov. 6:6). There are dozens of such similes in the Bible, but the purpose of this investigation is to identify creature-metaphor that has spiritual significance.

Dogs – Promoting Error
Under the Law, dogs were unclean animals and Jews could not have them for a house pet or use them for domestic purposes, such as tending sheep. Paul refers to the Jewish legalizers as dogs in Philippians 3:2-3. These men hounded Paul wherever he went and were bent on distorting

the gospel message of grace and leading people away from the truth. He consequently referred to these unclean and erroneous teachers as dogs.

Fox – Cunning, Crafty

In Luke 13:32, the Lord refers to the Herod Antipas, the Jewish tetrarch over the region of Galilee as being a fox. This inference meant that Herod had a sly and crafty character. Previously, the Lord had warned His disciples not to be influenced by *"the leaven of Herod"* (Mark 8:15). Herod, a Jew, was in cahoots with the Roman Empire, and was, therefore, a friend of the world (Jas. 4:4). In the case of Herod and those like him, love for God and His Word have been supplanted by the love for materialism, fame, and political ambition.

Serpent – Evil, Satan

John identifies Satan, the devil, as the serpent that was in Eden and deceived Eve into eating of the Tree of the Knowledge of Good and Evil (Gen. 3:1-8; Rev. 12:9). The Lord declared that Satan is the father of lies and that there is no truth in him (John 8:44). Paul exhorts the believer to put away all lying (Eph. 4:25). The Christian should not try to distort, change, or flavor the truth. That is what Satan does. The Lord wants us to state what "exactly conforms to reality" and expound it in love (Eph. 4:15).

The Lord Jesus used the historical event of Numbers 21 to teach His audience the essence of His gospel message. The Lord sent fiery serpents among the Israelites to punish them for complaining against Him – anyone bitten, died. After the Israelites repented and pleaded for mercy, God told Moses to set a bronze serpent on a pole in the midst of the camp, anyone looking at the serpent by faith would survive the deadly bit of the fiery serpents. The provision of the bronze serpent on a pole in Numbers 21 has its ultimate fulfillment in Christ hanging on the cross.

Bronze speaks of "fiery" judgments, while the serpent itself is a symbol of sin, and the lofty pole, prefigures Christ's cross. The imagery is astounding. God positionally condemned sin in the flesh (the energy of lawlessness) through the death of His Son on the cross. Because Christ rose from the grave, those trusting in Him receive eternal life in Him and the ability to overcome sin through the power of the Holy Spirit (John 3:16; Rom. 8:13).

Woman – Seduction, Wickedness

An angel calls the prophet Zechariah's attention to a basket (ephah) flying in the air (Zech. 5:5-9). The basket had a lead lid, which restrained a woman inside as two winged-women carried the basket towards Babylon. In this vision, an ephah (a dry measure used in common trade) and a woman (symbolizing the influences of systemized idolatry) are combined to illustrate the reason for Israel's captivity: prosperous business rooted in paganism. The woman representing this wickedness is being restrained within the basket by a heavy lid and is being carried back to Babylon by two angelic beings doing God's bidding (probably by unholy angels given the imagery). At the time of God's chastening, Israel was wicked and thoroughly tainted by heathen practices.

In God's original plan, woman was created to be Adam's helper and companion; however, she led Adam to disobey God in Eden. Likewise, as seen throughout Israel's history, foreign women often enticed Jewish men to depart from the Lord and to embrace false gods (e.g., Num. 25:6-8). So, although women are no more inherently wicked than men, a woman is used at times in the Bible to picture the influence of evil on men (i.e., to highlight the spiritual weakness of men to be seduced into error by sensual means). For this reason, we observe systems of evil being assigned to expressions such as *"the daughter of Zion"* and *"the daughter of Babylon"* (Zech. 2:7; Jer. 6:2).

The Lord Jesus employs a similar imagery in the fourth of His seven kingdom parables recorded in Matthew 13: A woman introduced leaven into good meal to corrupt the food of God's people (Matt. 13:33). However, God is quite capable of limiting the influence of wickedness among His people as shown by the heavy lead cover over the Zechariah's basket.

Other Earthly Creatures Summary
Dog – Promoting Error
Fox – Cunning, Crafty
Serpent – Evil, Satan
Woman – Seduction, Wickedness

Biblical Metaphor

Metals and Materials

Bronze – Judgment

Metaphorically speaking, bronze is used throughout Scripture to represent divine judgment, as intense heat was required to forge the alloy. This is why the feet of the Lord Jesus appear as flaming bronze in John's glorious vision of Christ, who poised to return to the Earth to render judgment upon the wicked: *"His feet were like burnished bronze, when it has been made to glow in a furnace"* (Rev. 1:15; NASB). Bronze speaks of God's judgment.

Another illustration of this understanding is found in the Bronze Altar in the tabernacle courtyard. This is where the sins of the Israelites would be judged under the Law. Its bronze construction and the constant offering of sacrifices on it conveyed God's righteous judgment in connection with human sin.

Both the length and the width of the Bronze Altar were to measure approximately seven and a half feet; it would stand four and a half feet tall with a bronze horn on each corner. It was to be constructed of acacia wood, which would then be overlaid with bronze. The rings for lifting and transporting the altar and all of its utensils, grates, and firepans were to be of bronze also. At this time, bronze was a forged amalgamation of copper and tin (later zinc would be used). The applied blood of the sacrifice on the horns of the Bronze Altar and the complete consuming of the sacrifice by fire on it speak of Christ's future sacrifice at Calvary. On the cross, Christ would be completely consumed by divine wrath while being judged for human sin. Consequently, the ever-smoking, ever-blood-stained Bronze Altar at the entrance to the tabernacle courtyard visibly announced to every Jew that the way of restoration was open. Through Christ, the way into God's presence is open for whomsoever will.

Gold – Purity, Holiness

The Lord Jesus rebuked the church at Laodicea because they were spiritually lethargic, materialistic, and lukewarm in their devotion to Him. He charges them:

> *You are wretched, miserable, poor, blind, and naked – I counsel you to buy from Me gold refined in the fire, that you may be rich; and white*

garments, that you may be clothed, that the shame of your nakedness may not be revealed (Rev. 3:17-18).

The radiant attire of the Bride of Christ in heaven will be her righteous acts (Rev. 19:8). The Lord warned the believers at Laodicea that they were, spiritually speaking, naked – they were not adoring themselves with righteous deeds. Likewise, they thought they were rich, but were spiritually bankrupt; they needed to receive pure gold from him, again speaking of doing what honors Christ and counts for eternity.

The Lord's own figurative language confirms that gold symbolizes purity, holiness, and righteousness. This is why all the furnishing in the tabernacle were to be of gold or a wood structure overlaid with gold – all was to project God's holy presence (Ex. 25-27).

For example, the Mercy Seat which set on the Ark of the Covenant was constructed of pure gold. Atoning blood of a goat and a bullock was sprinkled on and before the Mercy Seat by the high priest once a year on the Day of Atonement. The Ark of the Covenant was made of acacia wood and covered with pure gold. Ultimately, it would be Christ's blood presented before God that would provide propitiation for all human sin once and for all (Rom. 3:25; Heb. 9:11-15). Hence, the gold of the Mercy Seat and the Ark of the Covenant foreshadowed Christ's purity and holiness, while the humanity of Christ was symbolized by the wood in the ark.

Silver – Redemption

As previously noted in the explanation for the number *twenty*, silver symbolizes redemption in Scripture. The Lord Jesus was betrayed for thirty pieces of silver, which later the Pharisees referred to as "blood money" (Matt. 27:6). The pieces of silver were connected with the means of our ransom – Christ's own redeeming blood.

The baseplate of the tabernacle walls was constructed from the half shekel of silver that every Jewish man had to pay to affirm that they had been redeemed by the blood of the Passover lamb (Ex. 30:12). Their contribution indicated that their ransom had been fully paid and they were the Lord's people.

The boards and the rods that formed the walls of the tabernacle were made of wood overlaid with gold. Yet, the gold boards required a baseplate of silver sockets to stand erect (Ex. 26:15-28). Silver speaks of blood atonement under the Law (Ex. 30:16) and, more fully, of redemption in general. Thus, in the tabernacle, the gold and the wood combine to express the full deity and full humanity of Christ, while the silver speaks of Christ's redeeming blood.

At the command of the Lord, the prophet Hosea redeemed his lascivious wife Gomer for 15 pieces of silver and one-and-a-half homers of barley (Hos. 3:2). Gomer's infidelity pictured the spiritual adultery that Israel had committed against her husband, Jehovah. Gomer's restoration to Hosea, foreshadows Israel's future refinement and restoration with Jehovah in the Kingdom Age. The number twenty, silver, and barley all represent the idea of redemption in Scripture.

Wood – Humanity

The gold-covered acacia wood in the tabernacle furnishing (e.g., the Ark of the Covenant, the Table of Showbread, the Golden Altar of Incense) pictures Christ perfect humanity – He is the God incarnate. The bronze-covered wood in the Bronze Altar also pictures Christ's humanity (Ex. 25:10). But the emphasis in the Bronze Altar is not Christ's holy humanity, rather, that God's human sacrifice willing suffered His wrath.

Additionally, the ark that Noah was instructed to build pictures the safety that Christ offers all who will enter into Him by faith. Before the ark could be constructed, building materials were needed – gopher trees had to be cut down. The death of these trees pictured the humanity of Christ in that only through His sacrifice could spiritual life for man be secured. But since trees don't have blood, God is careful to apply some to the ark that we not miss the "type." The word *"pitch"* in Genesis 6:14 is most often translated "atonement" in the Old Testament. Prior to Calvary, man's sin could only be atoned (covered) by the blood of animals through sacrifices. The ark being pitched from within and without further shadows the future suffering and sacrifice of Christ. From His wounds redemptive blood would rudely and profusely coat his outer skin and then drip and splatter upon the ground. The word usage and the typology of Genesis 6 both convey the visage of a bleeding ark, thus picturing the suffering Savior at Calvary.

There was only one door into the ark (Gen. 6:16), and only God could shut it (Gen. 7:16) once all those who entered by faith were within. It would be God who judged the Earth for man's wickedness (Gen. 6:7); thus, the ark that Noah had built would know God's wrath. However, while the ark bore the judgment of almighty God, all the souls that were in the ark were kept safe from judgment. The Lord Jesus said He was the only door (John 10:1) and the only way (John 14:6), and He bore on a wooden cross the judgment of God for man's sin once and for all (Heb. 9:26-28, 10:9-18). As the flood waters increased, the ark floated higher and higher off the land. This pictures the believer's separation from the world that being in Christ demands (Gal. 6:14).

Isaiah prophesied that the coming Jewish Messiah would be both a "stem" ("shoot") and the "Root of Jesse": *"There shall come forth a Rod from the stem of Jesse, and a Branch shall grow out of his roots"* (Isa. 11:1). Isaiah predicted that the house of David would be in spiritual decline, but suddenly, out of this decaying branch, a fresh shoot of promise springs out. Hence, the Messiah, the *Rod* or *Branch* of David, will spring up from the *stem of Jesse,* but He will also be the *root cause* of this new life. Wood is again used in Scripture to speak of Christ's humanity, but He was much more – He was God incarnate.

Metals and Material Summary
Bronze – Judgment
Gold – Purity, Holiness
Silver – Redemption
Wood, Tree – Humanity or Christ's Cross

Colors

There were primarily four colors apparent in the tabernacle's curtains, tapestries, and in the priests' clothing and the high priest's Breast Plate: *purple, scarlet, white,* and *blue*. These four colors speak of Christ's offices, character, and essence. The writer of Hebrews informs us that Christ's own flesh was a veil (Heb. 10:19-20). Coverings in Scripture both reveal and conceal things. The Lord's flesh concealed the outshining glory of God but allowed His divine moral excellencies to be viewed by all (John 1:14).

The veil of the Lord's flesh is pictured in the inner veil of the tabernacle. This veil hung upon four pillars; each pillar consisted of wood (speaking of Christ's humanity) overlaid with gold (declaring Christ's deity). God dwelt on one side of this veil and man on the other. What a depiction of the Messiah – He would be both God and man. He was both the Son of David and David's Lord (Mark 12:35-37).

The veil was woven with four colored fabrics, the basic four colors of all the coverings throughout the tabernacle. William MacDonald comments:

> The four colors of materials in the tabernacle with their symbolic meanings also seem to fit the evangelists' fourfold presentation of the attributes of our Lord! ***Purple*** is an obvious choice for **Matthew**, the Gospel of the King. Judges 8:26 shows the regal nature of this color. ***Scarlet*** dye was derived in ancient times from crushing a cochineal worm. This suggests **Mark**, the Gospel of the bondservant, *"a worm and no man" (Ps. 22:6)*. ***White*** speaks of the righteous deeds of the saints (Rev. 19:8). **Luke** stresses the perfect humanity of Christ. ***Blue*** represents the sapphire dome we call the heavens (Ex. 24:10), an attractive representation of the Deity of Christ, a keynote in **John**.[6]

Purple is the color of royalty (Mark 15:17) and *white* the color of purity (Rev. 1:14, 6:11, 19:14). *Blue* is the heavenly color and is associated with God's things (Ex. 24:10; Num. 4:6-12). The Hebrew word for "worm" found Psalm 22:6 in the connections with Christ's suffering at Calvary is *tolaath*. The *tola* worm was smashed to yield a *scarlet*-colored dye. The reference was to the human brutality that Christ would suffer at Calvary, which climaxed with His crucifixion.

Two more noteworthy colors found in Scripture are *red* and *black*. While in a prophetic trance, John saw God the Father on His throne in heaven handover a scroll with seven seals to the Lamb, the Lord Jesus Christ. When the Lamb opened the second seal of the scroll a rider on a red horse was given a great sword and it was granted to him to take peace from the Earth (Rev. 6:3-4). We will refer to this rider as *War*, the converse of peace. He will cause much bloodshed during the Tribulation Period. The color *red* is associated with *war* and *bloodshed*.

John then describes the rider on a *black* horse that was released when Christ opened the third seal of the scroll; he carried a pair of scales in his hand (Rev. 6:5-6). He would masterfully use drought and pestilence to ensure widespread famine and starvation. But the rich, those following the Antichrist, would still enjoy the finer things of life. Accordingly, Job rightly identifies the color *black* with *death* (Job 3:5).

Additionally, Isaiah tells us that the light of God's essence defines what is true, righteous, and holy. What is not of God, by definition, forms darkness, that which is wickedness and sinful (Isa. 45:7).

Bible Numbers and Symbols

Color Summary
Black – Death, Sin
Blue – Heaven
Purple – Royalty
Red – War, Bloodshed
Scarlet – Humility, Service
White – Purity, Righteousness

Miscellaneous
Barley – Redemption

The Lord commanded the prophet Hosea to go to the slave market and to purchase his lascivious and estranged wife. Despite the heartache that she had caused Hosea, he obeyed the Lord and bought (redeemed) her for fifteen pieces of silver and a homer and half-homer of barley (about forty-five bushels). Both silver and barley are used to symbolize redemption throughout Scripture. For instance, we first find Ruth, the Moabite, gleaning barley in the fields of her future kinsman-redeemer, Boaz (Ruth 2:3, 3:15). She realized the special measure of grace that had been shown to her and thanked Boaz for his generosity (Ruth 2:10).

Following the Jewish custom, the Lord Jesus would have broken an unleavened barley loaf at the Passover Feast the night before His crucifixion (Lev. 23:6-14; Luke 22:14-20). The breaking of this bread pictured the abuse that He would personally suffer to accomplish His redemptive work at Calvary on our behalf.

Basket – Trade, Commerce

As previously noted in the discussion concerning the symbolic use of a woman in Scripture, the basket flying through the air in Zechariah's vision was common ephah (Zech. 5:5-9). This basket was used as a dry measure in common trade and thus, is a symbol of human business affairs. In this vision, an ephah, in conjunction with the woman (who symbolizes idolatry), are combined to illustrate the reason for Israel's captivity: prosperous business rooted in paganism.

Circle, Ring – Eternity

John saw a circular rainbow around God's heavenly throne (Rev. 4:3). The rainbow was given to Noah as a symbol of God's covenant with him (Gen. 9:13). The circle, a ring, or a wheel represents eternity –

it continues without end (Ezek. 1:16). Therefore, the circular rainbow about God's throne is an eternal testimony that God always keeps His word and fulfills His promises! And, though man has grieved God severely throughout human history, He has kept His promise to Noah of not destroying the Earth again by water, even to this day.

Earth, Field, Land – Israel

Figuratively speaking, especially in the realm of prophecy, *the Earth* or *the land* or *the field*, refers to the land of Israel. Jacob, was renamed "Israel," as the nation came about through him. In the dream, God spoke to Jacob and reconfirmed the covenant He had made with Abraham and Isaac. Jacob was promised seed that would be as the dust of the earth (Gen. 28:14). Isaac was promised descendants as numerous as the stars of heaven (Gen. 26:4). Abraham, in whom the covenant was first established, was promised both (Gen. 22:17). Why the difference? Because Isaac represents the resurrected Christ who has inherited a heavenly land with heavenly promises, and Jacob represents the expansion of the nation of Israel, which will inherit an earthly land and earthly promises during the Millennium.

In the fifth of the seven Kingdom Parables found in Matthew 13:44, the Lord refers to His covenant people, the Jews, as a special treasure. This treasure had been previously lost to Him through willful idolatry, but He had come to the earth through the incarnation to see them again. He found His treasure again and offer the Jewish people the good news of the Kingdom message (Matt. 4:17). But they rejected it and its Messenger – Christ, so the Lord again buried them in the land and went to the cross to legally purchase them by His own blood. In a coming day (in the Kingdom Age), He will return to find them again and then they will be restored to Him forever. He will rule over them in the land of Israel.

It is noted that the false prophet, the third beast described by John in the book of Revelation, rises out of *the land*. The false prophet, will likely be a well-known Jew from Israel, who will cause others to give honor to the Antichrist by performing miracles. He will deceive many into worshiping the beast, and thus honoring Satan (Rev. 13:14-15).

Eyes – Seeing, Knowing

The prophet Ezekiel receives a spectacular vision of God's mobile throne which reset on four-unidirectional wheels that had rims full eyes (Ezek. 1:17-19). The description of the wheels expresses functionality rather than mechanical design, as the laws of nature do not apply to this chariot. The wheels connected the throne of God to the Earth and hence the rims being full of eyes symbolize God's omniscience in the affairs of men:

> *For the eyes of the Lord run to and fro throughout the whole Earth, to show Himself strong on behalf of those whose heart is loyal to Him. In this you have done foolishly; therefore from now on you shall have wars* (2 Chron. 16:9).

> *The eyes of the Lord are in every place, keeping watch on the evil and the good* (Prov. 15:3).

God is intimately aware of all that happens on the Earth and governs all the affairs of men to accomplish His purposes, especially for His own people. There is nothing left to chance, nothing that catches God by surprise – He sees all, knows all, and controls all things (Ps. 33:18; 1 Pet. 3:12).

Accordingly, the Lord Jesus, the Lamb in heaven, is described by John as having seven eyes (Rev. 5:6). An *eye* represents *sight*, we understand this description to speak of the Lord's divine omniscience – He knows and sees all things.

Fire – Judgment, Purification

One of the first times that fire is used as both a means of and emblem of judgment is when God destroyed several wicked cities in the Jordan valley (including Sodom and Gomorrah). Fire fell from heaven to completely consume these cities (Gen. 19:24).

The next time that fire is used in a symbolic way is when we witness Abraham and Isaac ascend a mountain in the land Moriah to offer God a burnt sacrifice, which is to be Isaac (Gen. 22). Abraham (representing God the Father) is carrying the fire and the knife up the mount, both are symbols of judgment in Scripture. Isaac, a young man, bore the wood for the fire. Prior to being judged by the Father at Calvary, the Lord Jesus had shouldered His crossbeam until physically unable. Isaac inquired about a missing animal for sacrifice. Abraham responded that *"God will provide for Himself the lamb,"* and He did some 2000 years later in the Lord Jesus. John the Baptist heralded the Lord Jesus as *"The Lamb of God who takes away the sin of the world!"* (John 1:29).

Other examples of fire being used as symbol of judgment or purification include Leviticus 10:2; Numbers 16:35; Psalm 12:6; Matthew 3:11, 13:39-40, and 25:41.

Harlot – Humanize Religion

John informs us that the Antichrist's political and economic system is identified with Babylon and will be destroyed by Christ at His second advent (Rev. 18). The religious aspect of this system, which the Antichrist will use to gain control of the world, will actually be eliminated by the Antichrist himself during the middle portion of the Tribulation Period (Rev. 17). This event coincides with what is called "the Abomination of Desolation." At that time, the Antichrist will no longer tolerate the one-world religion he helped create; he will demand to be worshiped as god himself (2 Thess. 2:4-7).

Initially, John describes a sumptuously dressed harlot riding a beast that was previously identified as the Antichrist (Rev. 13:1-10; 17:1-4). But half way through the Tribulation Period, the Antichrist will destroy her, the last religious system of humanism, which began with Nimrod in Babylon of old: *"MYSTERY, BABYLON THE GREAT, THE MOTHER OF HARLOTS AND OF THE ABOMINATIONS OF THE EARTH"* (Rev. 17:5). This religious system is responsible for the death of millions of God's people throughout the course of human history. The harlot, as John describes her, is *"drunk with the blood of the saints"* (Rev. 17:6).

Under God's Law for Israel, a harlot, a woman who sells herself for sexual favors, was despised by those loyal to Jehovah. Metaphorically speaking, this meaning carries into the spiritual realm also (e.g., Jas. 4:4). The harlot of Revelation 17 is the apex of religious humanism, which will be completely judged. She persecutes and slaughters God's people in the name of religion and she sells herself to do what God hates. Likewise, we should hate what God passionately loathes.

Head - Authority

Given Daniel's prophecies (Dan. 7 and 8), and John's description of the Antichrist in Revelation 17, we understanding that his seven heads represent seven kingdoms, and that the ten horns represent kings within the final kingdom in which the Antichrist will rule over. This is why the crowns on the beast depicting the Antichrist are on the ten horns (Rev. 13:1-10), but the crowns are on the seven heads of the dragon in Revelation 12, who represents Satan. Satan has been permitted to and will be permitted to control seven world empires in human history (John 12:31, 14:30). Six have past, but one is still coming. The seventh is the one that Antichrist will rule over to accomplish Satan's agenda.

Paul uses the word *head* in a figurative way to express the authority that God the Father has over God the Son, though being divine, they are equals. In the same way, man is to have authority over the woman in creation order, though God views equality among the two genders (1 Cor. 11:3). To not submit to this order, as unto Christ, causes shame to one's head (1 Cor. 11:4-5); this ultimately results in disdain of the Church's head – Christ (Eph. 1:22; Tit. 2:4-5).

Horn – Power

John describes the Lamb, the Lord Jesus Christ, as having *seven* horns before the throne of God in Revelation 5:6. It is not likely that the Lord Jesus Christ will physically look like this in heaven. Rather, the seven horns symbolically represent His divine omnipotence, as *seven* is God's number of spiritual *perfection*, while a *horn* represents *power*.

While ascending the mount in the land of Moriah, Isaac had asked his father, Abraham, *"Where is the lamb for a burnt offering?"* (Gen. 22:7. Abraham responded by saying, *"My son, God will provide for Himself the lamb of a burnt offering"* (Gen. 22:8). Isaac was not to be the sacrifice offered to the Lord at this juncture, rather, God provided Himself an offering for sacrifice – a ram caught by its horns (Gen. 22:13).

Many male animals use their horns/antlers to protect themselves when attacked, or to mark and then to defend their territory. It is no surprise then that Scripture uses a *horn* to symbolize power and strength. With God's provision of the ram for sacrifice, the type of the Lord Jesus is transferred from Isaac to the one caught by its horns and would suffer death. Correspondingly, the Lord laid aside His glory and position in heaven to become a man in order to be a humble substitute for us at Calvary (Phil. 2:6-8). Meekness is "power in control" and is represented by the restrained ram. Just as Isaac did not use his youthful strength to escape Abraham's efforts to sacrifice him, the Lord Jesus did not use His power to escape His Father's will for Him at Calvary.

Both Daniel and John refer to the Antichrist and his ten kings under him as "horns" to depict the authority and power that they will share for a brief time (i.e., during the Tribulation Period; Dan. 7:7-25; Rev. 17:12).

Lampstand – Testimony

The Golden Lampstand was made from a single piece of beaten gold and was the only source of light in the tabernacle. The Lampstand's light represents the Holy Spirit's perfect testimony of truth centered in Christ (2 Cor. 1:20; Rev. 4:5, 19:10). The flowing olive oil supplied to each of the seven burning wicks represents the perfect enabling power of the Holy Spirit to accomplish the will of God (Zech. 4:6). The Lampstand typifies the Person and work of Christ; consequently, each of the seven lamps was to be positioned in such a way as to cast their full light before the Lampstand (v. 4).

The Holy Spirit's work in the Church now, as in Israel then, was and is completely dependent on Christ. Every ray of light that radiates God's glory in the life of believers today flows from Christ as empowered by the Holy Spirit. This is why believers are not to hid their lamp, their testimony for Christ, under a basket; rather, it is to shine brightly to a world that desperately needs to see the grace of God in Christ (Matt. 5:13-16).

As mentioned in the *star* discussion, the seven lampstands about Christ in Revelation 1, represented the testimonies of seven churches in Asia Minor in John's day. Most of these churches received praised from the Lord, but two did not, and five were admonished to repent of sinful attitudes that were hindering their testimony of Christ. For example, the church at Ephesus, though they had good works and sound doctrine, eventually lost their lampstand (their church testimony) because their love for Christ waned (Rev. 2:2-5). He no longer had first place in their affections. No doubt, these saints continued in form for some time, but they did not have the joy and power of His presence among them – this is a deathblow to any local church.

Mountain – Kingdoms

Having indicted Israel's rulers and false prophets and foretold God's chastening calamity coming to the region, the prophet Micah transitions to a positive theme of hope in chapter 4. He reveals the tenor of the Kingdom Age (4:1-8), the events directly preceding it (4:9-5:1), and the King who will reign over it (5:2-15). Micah prefaces this section by stating that the Kingdom of God, depicted as a mountain, would come *"in the latter days"* (Micah 4:1). Then *"the mountain of the Lord's house"* (Micah 4:2; Isa. 2:2; Dan. 2:44-45) will be above all mountains of the Earth (i.e., God's kingdom will have worldwide acknowledgment and supremacy). Isaiah and Micah were contemporaries, and both prophets foretold God's glorious mountain on Earth, speaking of Messiah's earthly kingdom.

When metaphorically applied in Scripture, mountains are used to symbolize governmental authorities or kingdoms (Rev. 17:9-10). There was one instance during the latter days of the Lord's ministry in Decapolis that His divine essence was permitted to shine out of Him to picture exactly what Isaiah is alluding to in verses 2-5. The event is what we commonly call the "transfiguration." Matthew describes it:

> *Now after six days Jesus took Peter, James, and John his brother, led them up on a high mountain by themselves; and He was transfigured before them. His face shone like the sun, and His clothes became as white as the light* (Matt. 17:1-2).

In the preceding verse, the Lord Jesus had said, *"Assuredly, I say to you, there are some standing here who shall not taste death till they see the Son of Man coming in His kingdom"* (Matt. 16:28). For a brief moment the disciples were given a foretaste of the coming kingdom; they saw the intrinsic glory of Christ in a measure.

One can only imagine how the glory of the Lord appeared on a high mountain in a remote region and apparently at night (Luke 9:32-37). The transfiguration foretells a future day when Christ will rule the world and His intrinsic glory will be seen throughout the Earth. When that kingdom is established, the word of God will go forth from Jerusalem and all nations will come to *"the house of the God of Jacob"* to see the glory of God and to worship Him (Isa. 2:3, 60:14, 66:10-18; Zech. 14:16-21). Indeed, the whole Earth will be full of God's glory (Isa. 2:13, 2:2, 62:1-7).

Oil – The Holy Spirit

As mentioned in the Lampstand discussion, the pure flowing olive oil supplied to each of the seven burning wicks of the Golden Lampstand represents the perfect enabling power of the Holy Spirit to accomplish the will of God. The prophet Zechariah later verifies that through the power of the Holy Spirit (the olive oil), the high priest Joshua and the governor Zerubbabel (the two olive trees in the vision) would rebuild the temple in Jerusalem (Zech. 4). The temple would be a testimony (a lampstand) of Jehovah's greatness among the nations. Olive oil is a clear type of the Holy Spirit in Scripture: *"This is the word of the Lord to Zerubbabel: 'Not by might nor by power, but by My Spirit,' Says the Lord of hosts"* (Zech. 4:6).

Rainbow – Promise, Covenant

God responded to Noah's burnt offerings by giving him a visible sign to accompany His new covenant with him. The rainbow would be a token of God's promise never to judge the Earth again by a flood. After the flood, many things in man's world changed. It would rain regularly, there would be direct sunlight, and man would eat meat (but not the blood). The Earth would have seasons and polar caps. The flood radically changed the Earth!

The ongoing symbol of God's promise to Noah, would be the product of both storm and light and would be hung in heaven for all to see and appreciate. Thus, the rainbow is a portrait of God's unfailing grace. To the believer God's grace and peace settle our hearts during life's storms – for He will not test us above what we are able to bear without providing the way of escape (1 Cor. 10:13). To the unbeliever, the rainbow is an invitation to find peace with God and escape the wrath to come. *"For the grace of God that brings salvation has appeared to all men"* (Tit. 2:11).

River – Peace

Genesis 1 records all God's creative work as pertaining to mankind on the Earth. This included a lush garden called Eden and a river that flowed out of Eden and water the whole land (Gen. 2:10-14). God rested from His work for all was good. Our first parents had a perfect environment to labor for and to enjoy fellowship with God.

When God rested from His work, the whole world enjoyed the blessing and refreshment of God's presence and blessing. There is a connection between the one river out of Eden and God's rest. Consequently, a river is used throughout Scripture to convey the truth that all peace and blessing originates with God then flows out to others.

Moses smote a rock to provide flowing water to the children of Israel in the desert to save their lives. The Lord likened the blessings of the Holy Spirit in a believer's life to a river of flowing water (John 7:37-39). Then when the Lord returns to Earth at the end of the Tribulation Period, He will split the Mount of Olives, and a river of living water will flow towards the east and the west symbolizing that world peace and rest has come (Zech. 14:8).

Finally, in the eternal state, after the present Earth has been destroyed, there shall be a *"pure river of water of life"* flowing out from the throne of God forever and ever (Rev. 22:1). Until man sinned, God rested, and His peace flowed out of His presence upon the whole Earth. After God had completely dealt with sin through the work of Christ, all will be at rest again forever!

Seas – The Nations

Metaphorically speaking we understand that seas represent the nations (Rev. 17:1, 15). The Millennial Kingdom of Christ will begin directly after *The Judgment of Nations* at the conclusion of the Tribulation Period. The Lord Jesus taught about this judgment in the seventh of the Kingdom Parables found in Matthew 13:47-50. In that parable, the Lord casts a net into the sea (i.e., into the nations) and sorts through that which is caught. Those who did not follow the Antichrist are separated from those who did.

The "good" are permitted into His kingdom; the "bad" are committed to eternal judgment. The net represents the influence of the kingdom gospel message that will be preached worldwide during the Tribulation Period (Matt. 24:14). This message consists of a warning not to worship the Antichrist and a declaration that judgment of the wicked and Christ's kingdom are coming soon (Rev. 14:6-12). The fish represent the living Gentiles who are saved during the Tribulation Period.

As previously discussed, the Antichrist is described as a beast rising out of the sea (Rev. 13:1). This means that he will first appear from out of the nations and not from Israel.

Stars – Angels, Messengers

John describes the vision that he received of Christ glorified and standing in the midst of the seven lampstands, while holding seven stars in His hand (Rev. 1:9-16). The Lord informs John the meaning of what he saw:

> *The mystery of the seven stars which you saw in My right hand, and the seven golden lampstands: The seven stars are the angels of the seven churches, and the seven lampstands which you saw are the seven churches* (Rev. 1:20).

The Lord explained that the seven lampstands were the testimonies of seven churches in Asia Minor that He would personally address through seven divine messengers, generally believed to be angels. Revelation 2 and 3 then recorded the contents of the seven letters delivered to each of these seven churches. We again find that a *star* represents an angel in Revelation 9:1. Given this understanding, it seems likely that Satan led a third of the stars in heaven (a third of all angels) in rebellion against God (Rev. 12:4).

Sword, Knife – Judgment
Like fire, a sword or a knife is used to represent judgment in Scripture. We have just noticed that Abraham was carrying both emblems of judgment while ascending the mount to offer Isaac as an offering (Gen. 22:6).

John describes the visage of Christ glorified in heaven and poised to return to the Earth to vindicate His name in Revelation 1. The description is full of metaphor in order to better emphasize Christ's disposition and character. John describes a sharp two-edged sword coming out of the Lord's mouth (Rev. 1:16, 19:15). At His second advent, Christ will simply speak judgment against His enemies and none will be able to stand against Him. The prophet Zechariah describes this future scene in detail (Zech. 14). This symbolizes that His method of judging the Antichrist and all that align with him would through His spoken words.

Wheat – Resurrection Life
After her first day of gleaning barley (with the provisions permitted by Boaz), Ruth derived a five-day supply for both her and Naomi. When Naomi saw the unusual amount of gleaned grain for a single day's effort, she was astonished (Ruth 2:18). Recognizing God's providential care, she inquired from Ruth where she had gleaned. Ruth then told Naomi the wonderful events of the day and how a man named Boaz showed much kindness to her.

Naomi knew Boaz, and in fact; Boaz was kin of her dead husband Elimelech. Understanding the potential of obtaining redemption through her kinsman Boaz, she instructs Ruth to heed his invitation and return only to his fields to glean and also to remain among his maidens (Ruth 2:21-22). It is doubtful that Ruth, being a stranger in Israel, fully understood what Naomi was talking about (i.e., Levitical Laws pertaining to redemption). Regardless, she obeyed the instruction of her mother-in-law and labored hard from the commencement of the barley harvest to the conclusion of the wheat harvest; about seven or eight weeks (Ruth 2:23).

Barley was the poor man's grain; wheat was the better grain and hence, three times more expensive (Rev. 6:6). Regardless, the two grains are connected, with barley representing redemption and wheat the fuller benefits of redemption, including resurrection life. Both grains are tied together in the Levitical Feasts. Barley was the grain used in the unleavened bread of Passover and what was waved before the Lord in First Fruits, but wheat was the grain used in the wave loaves offered to the Lord at the Feast of Pentecost (Lev. 23:15-22). The Feast of Weeks occurred during the wheat harvest (about seven weeks after the barley was reaped) and marked the end of the spring harvest time.

This was the only time throughout the entire year that leavened bread was presented to the Lord. F. Duane Lindsey describes the process for producing the two leaven loaves:

> The bread was leavened by placing in the dough a lump of leaven (i.e., sourdough) from bread of the preceding barley harvest, thus reemphasizing the close connection between the barley and the wheat harvest, and the festivals associated with them.[7]

Recall that the resurrected Lord Jesus was represented in the barley wave sheaf at The Feast of Firstfruits. The grain from this sheaf was later ground and used to create sourdough. Fifty days later, a lump of the barley sourdough was placed into the freshly ground wheat flour to create the two wave loaves, thus, the wave sheaf and the wheat harvest that followed are connected in the two loaves. Obviously, there is no leaven in Christ, the Wave Sheaf, but believers united with Him (the Church) still have a leavened nature within them. This is nullified by the invisible heat of the oven in the same way that the indwelling Holy Spirit invisibly controls and empowers believers. Barley pictures redemption in the Bible, but wheat typifies the blessings of resurrection life that the believer has in Christ (Matt. 13:24-25, 38; John 12:24). In Christ, we receive power over sin through the Holy Spirit!

Miscellaneous Summary
Barley – Redemption
Basket – Trade, Commerce
Circle, Ring – Eternity, Security
Earth, Field – Israel
Eyes – Seeing, Knowing
Fire – Judgment, Purification
Harlot – Humanize Religion
Head – Authority
Horn – Power
Lampstand – Testimony
Mountain – Kingdom
Oil – The Holy Spirit
Rainbow – Promise, Covenant
River – Peace
Sea – The Nations
Stars – Angels, Messengers
Sword, Knife – Judgment
Wheat – Resurrection Life

A Triune God in Metaphor

A triune God created all that was created. Paul often wrote of the Trinity, *"Yet for us there is one God, the Father, of whom are all things, and we for Him; and one Lord Jesus Christ, through whom are all things, and through whom we live"* (1 Cor. 8:6). *"The grace of the Lord Jesus Christ, and the love of God, and the communion of the Holy Spirit be with you all"* (2 Cor. 13:14). Paul understood that our existence, our salvation, and our fellowship is integrally connected with a triune God.

In the same way, the Lord Jesus commanded that all those who had believed His Gospel message be baptized *"in the name of the Father and of the Son and of the Holy Spirit"* (Matt. 28:19). God is three individuals in one entity. All three are God, eternal, and equal, though Scripture does reveal a distinction in personality and in roles, but not in divine attributes or holy character.

One of the clearest references to the Trinity in the Old Testament is found in Isaiah 48:13-17. Notice that the One speaking in these verses is the Creator of all things and Controller of the future. His is the second person of the Godhead, as He refers to God the Father and God the Spirit as equals:

> *"**Come near to Me**, hear this: I have not spoken in secret from the beginning; from the time that it was, I was there. And now the Lord God* [God the Father] *and His Spirit* [the Holy Spirit] *have sent Me* [God the Son]*." Thus says the Lord, your Redeemer, the Holy One of Israel*: *"I am the Lord your God, who teaches you to profit, who leads you by the way you should go"* (Isa. 48:16-17).

This passage unfolds to us God's great plan of salvation for humanity: God the Father and the Holy Spirit sent the Son to earth to become the Redeemer, the Holy One of Israel. "The Holy One" was a title the demons used to refer to Christ while speaking with Him during His earthly sojourn (Mark 1:24; Luke 4:34). Moreover, the Redeemer, the Person speaking, clearly identifies Himself as the Lord, the God of Israel.

New Testament Scripture further explains this interaction within the Godhead: The Lord Jesus stated that He had come to the earth to do the

Father's will (Luke 22:42; John 10:18, 14:31). The angel Gabriel announced to Mary that she would conceive and give birth to the Lord Jesus through the overshadowing power of the Holy Spirit (Luke 1:35). The Father sent the Son, and the Holy Spirit enabled the incarnation, so that the Son of God could come to the Earth and be born of a virgin. These same roles within the Trinity are also witnessed in biblical typology.

Scripture is especially saturated with "types" of Christ. These give evidence of Christ, but are obviously not Him. There is no perfect "type" or "pattern," or it would be the real thing. Therefore, all types, foreshadows, symbols, analogies, and patterns are inadequate to express fully and completely every aspect of each Person and the work that each does within the Godhead.

God the Father

In the Bible, a type of God the Father is seen in father Abraham (Gen. 22). Abraham is willing to offer his only son Isaac for a sacrifice, just as God the Father was willing to send and offer His only Son for a sin sacrifice on our behalf. Later, when it is time for Isaac to rule over all that Abraham had, we read, *"Abraham gave all that he had to Isaac"* (Gen. 25:5). Likewise, the Father has committed all that He has into His Son's hands; Christ will inherit and rule over all things (1 Cor. 15:24-28; Heb. 1:4, 8).

God the Son

Types of Christ in the Old Testament are usually seen in both *people* and *objects*. Many of these types have already been discussed previously in this book. Objects include: Noah's ark, a smiting stone, a smitten stone, a rock of offense, a cornerstone, a stumbling stone, a foundational rock, a rod, a door, an arm, a shepherd, a lamb, a mountain, a veil, a bronze serpent on a pole, etc. People representing some aspect of Christ personage or work would include: Melchizedek, Isaac, Joseph, Ben-Oni/Benjamin, Moses, the high priest, Joshua, David, and Elisha. These are all objects or people being used to accomplish God's work, which pictures Christ performing the Father's will.

The Holy Spirit

The Holy Spirit is generally depicted in *active* fluids: flowing olive oil (Zech. 4), blowing wind (John 3), seven flames of fire (Rev. 4), and rushing water (John 7). The Holy Spirit, in these types, is not visibly seen doing the Father's will, but rather enabling and accomplishing the task at hand in a powerful and invisible fashion. This operation of the Holy Spirit is clearly seen in Genesis 1:2, *"The Spirit of God moved upon the face of the waters."* Here the Holy Spirit is described as "moving" in the presence of the formless water (i.e., energizing what was lifeless and formless).

God the Master Potter

Although God is often identified by plural nouns and pronouns, He is a singular entity and therefore is usually addressed as and revealed in a singular fashion. For example, the prophet Jeremiah likened God to a Potter who was working to shape Israel into a stunning vessel that all the nations would admire (Jer. 18:1-6). But because Israel resisted His efforts, like unworkable clay, God had to set them aside.

God then took up a second lump of clay to shape; this is likely a reference to the Church. After it is fashioned, as only God can, He will return to work with the first lump of marred clay, the Jewish nation (Rom. 11:25). In time, the divine Potter will put that which was discarded back on His wheel and form it into a useful vessel of His choosing. The shaping of the Jewish nation will be completed during the Tribulation Period when they will be infused with the life of Christ and be restored to Him forever.

One cannot read this portion of Scripture without contemplating God's mysterious ways in each of our lives. When an individual, a lump of clay, so to speak, yields to the gospel message, the molding process begins; until then the clay is marred by sin and cannot be fashioned into a vessel of honor. When a potter sets a lump of softened clay upon the wheel in order to make something of it, the first thing he or she does is to poke into the center of the clay with his or her hand or some other instrument. This reminds us that God molds us from the inside out; He starts by cleansing and shaping the heart. Circumstances in this life then supply the Potter's wheel with the motion and energy to assist the Master's hand in molding our hearts to the pattern of Christ-likeness.

Mysterious are God's ways! How is it that He can incorporate both human submission and rebellion into His sovereign design, causing all events to bring about His glory? Before creation, God previewed the corridors of time, considered all the possible permutations of natural cause and effect as well as the future choices of cognitive beings, and made sovereign choices to bless humanity in time and glorify His name throughout time and eternity. As only a triune God existed when the plan of redemption was devised, the plan is solely His – it originated in His mind and He deserves all the glory for it (1 Pet. 1:17-21). God's choices ensure that humanity will receive the greatest possible blessing and that He will obtain the most glory as a result.

We presently live in the latter days of the Church Age. Paul foretold that this timeframe would be marked by a general departure from sound doctrine by the professing Church. Many in Christendom today profess Christ, but do not truly know Him. The Lord Jesus said, that many of those calling Him "Lord," who have done things in His name, and who even know a lot about Him, were never saved; these souls will suffer eternal judgment (Matt. 7:21-23).

In such days of deception and declension, what could be more necessary than true believers exploring the fathomless Word of God and be transformed by it into the likeness of Christ (2 Cor. 3:18; Heb. 4:12)? The Master Potter desires to shape and mold each of His children into something spectacular for the praise of His glory (Eph. 1:12). My prayer is that the study of biblical numerology and metaphor has excited you to pursue a deeper study of God's Word. God desires us to find and appreciate these spiritual gemstones within the deeper layers of Scripture, but He will not force anyone to dig for them! *"Be diligent to present yourself approved to God, a worker who does not need to be ashamed, rightly dividing the word of truth"* (2 Tim. 2:15).

Endnotes

1. Ed. F Vallowe, *Biblical Mathematics – Keys to Scripture Numerics* (Ed. F. Vallowe Evangelistics Association; Forest Park, GA; 1991 – 15th printing, p. 233
2. N. L. Geisler, "New Testament Manuscripts" in *Baker Encyclopedia Of Christian Apologetics* (Baker Books, Grand Rapids, MI; 2002), p. 532
3. F. W. Grant, *Spiritual Law in the Natural World* (Loizeaux Brothers, Neptune N.J.; 1891 – first printing), chp. 5
4. Louis A. Barbieri, Jr., *The Bible Knowledge Commentary* by Dallas Seminary (Victor Books, Wheaton, IL; 1983), p. 18
5. Ivan Panin, *The Shorter Works of Ivan Panin: Bible Numerics* (Reprinted by the British Israel Ass., Vancouver, B.C.; 1934), pp. 30-31
6. William MacDonald, *Believer's Bible Commentary* (Thomas Nelson Publishers, Nashville, TN; 1989), p. 1198
7. F. Duane Lindsey & Dallas Theological Seminary, *The Bible Knowledge Commentary: An Exposition of the Scriptures* (Victor Books, Wheaton, IL; 1983-1985), p. 207

OLD TESTAMENT
Devotional Commentary Series

- **Christ-Centered Exposition**
- **Life-Changing Application**
- **Fourteen Volumes**
- **Over 5,400 Pages**
- **Nearly 200 Contributors**

The primary purpose for studying God's Word is to know the Lord and learn how to please Him. The aim of a devotional commentary is to help the reader pause and consider the deeper, life-related implications of the portion being read. What is God telling us about His character, emotions and attributes? How is His plan of salvation being displayed? How should we respond to His Word? Today, the Christian community sits atop a vast array of written resources, many of which have been penned by those who have gone to be with Christ. Though some of these books are out of print, they still display a relevance to current issues while maintaining a deeply devotional viewpoint, sadly lacking in much of today's Christian literature. This *OT Devotional Commentary Series* captures some of the richest gleanings of nearly two hundred time-honored authors whose goal was sound biblical exposition that would magnify Christ and lead to godly living. Each volume contains dozens of brief devotions. This permits the reader to use the series as a daily devotional or as a reference source for deeper study.

— *Warren Henderson*

A New Testament Journey
May We Serve Christ!

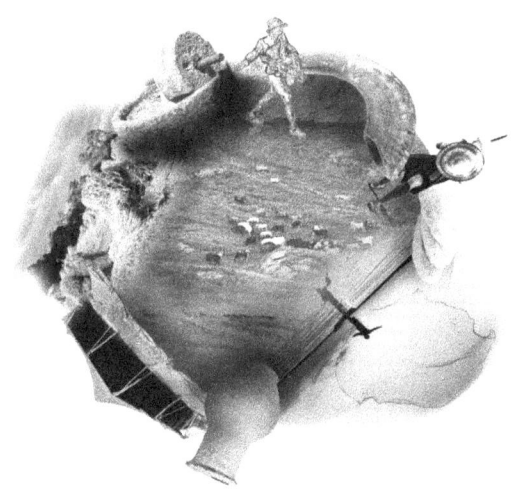

WARREN HENDERSON

At this moment, each of us is as close to the Lord Jesus Christ as we desire to be. Our patient Savior is always ready to assist anyone genuinely seeking Him and desiring to serve Him in his or her appointed capacity and calling. Through His Word and His Spirit, God aids a true seeker every step of the way into a deeper knowledge of Himself and His purposes. *May We Serve Christ? – A New Testament Journey* draws practical application from Scripture to convict, to confront, and to encourage us to *"press toward the goal for the prize of the upward call of God in Christ Jesus"* (Phil. 3:14.). There is a Savior to know, a work to do, a calling to be fulfilled, a race to run, and a higher experience with God to be enjoyed! — Warren Henderson

May We See Christ – An Old Testament Journey is a sequential study of Scripture containing 366 two-page devotions (758 pages). Besides the plain language of the Old Testament, God has employed a variety of types, symbols, and allegories in a complementary fashion to teach us about His Son. With the light of New Testament truth and the illuminating assistance of the Holy Spirit, we are able to understand and appreciate these fascinating Old Testament pictures. All of God's written Word speaks of Christ to some degree as He is the main emphasis of Scripture. Accordingly, the best reason to embark on this one-year journey is to more clearly see, know, and love Christ. May the Lord richly bless your daily contemplations of the Savior as you expectantly peer into God's oracles and witness the glory of His Son. — Warren Henderson

www.ingramcontent.com/pod-product-compliance
Lightning Source LLC
Chambersburg PA
CBHW070644050426
42451CB00008B/299